Being a Christian Friend

How Christian friendship can help you draw closer to God

Kristen Johnson Ingram

Judson Press ® Valley Forge

BEING A CHRISTIAN FRIEND
Copyright © 1985
Judson Press, Valley Forge, PA 19482-0851
Second Printing, 1988

All rights reserved. No part of this publication may be reproduced, stored in a retrieval system, or transmitted in any form or by any means, electronic, mechanical, photocopying, recording, or otherwise, without the prior permission of the copyright owner, except for brief quotations included in a review of the book.

Unless otherwise indicated, Bible quotations in this volume are from the HOLY BIBLE New International Version, copyright © 1978, New York International Bible Society. Used by permission.

Other versions of the Bible quoted in this book are:

The Holy Bible, King James Version.

The Revised Standard Version of the Bible copyrighted 1946, 1952 © 1971, 1973 by the Division of Christian Education of the National Council of the Churches of Christ in the U.S.A., and used by permission.

The New English Bible. Copyright © The Delegates of the Oxford University Press and The Syndics of the Cambridge University Press 1961, 1970.

The Jerusalem Bible, copyright © 1966 by Darton, Longman and Todd, Ltd. and Doubleday and Company, Inc. Used by permission of the publisher.

Library of Congress Cataloging in Publication Data
Ingram, Kristen, J.
  Being a Christian friend.
  1. Friendship—Religious aspects—Christianity.
I. Title.
BV4647.F7154 1985   241'.676   85-5583
ISBN 0-8170-1084-X

The name JUDSON PRESS is registered as a trademark in the U.S. Patent Office.
Printed in the U.S.A.

*For my friend, Shirley Oliver Stuelpnagel,
whose love and faithfulness are not
measurable by earthly standards*

Contents

1. What Is Friendship? 7
2. Friends in Christ 9
3. Making Friends 17
4. Times and Speeds in Friendship 23
5. The Taming of the Tongue 37
6. Healthy Self-Esteem—And Myths About Self-Love 51
7. How to Tell a Friend from an Alligator 61
8. Some Friendships in the Old Testament 73
9. Friends of the New Covenant 83
10. Personal Relationship with Jesus Christ:
    The Ultimate Friendship 95
11. Prayer Partners and Spiritual Friends 105

1

What Is Friendship?

Someone once gave me a birthday card that asked in red and gold Old English script, "What is a friend?"

The answers it gave were sentimental and shallow. It described a friend as "someone who's always there with a ready smile," "a comfortable place to turn when the world is dark," and "the one who cares when all others have deserted." The person described on the card's three little pages sounded like a cross between a comforting massage cushion, a flashlight, and a jolly insurance agent.

Friendships aren't that simple, nor are they always comfortable. They are sometimes abrasive and often complicated. The reasons for starting them may not be the reasons they continue, and the people in them may not even be able to explain them. In fact, perhaps in every relationship there's always an indescribable quality, an X factor, that can't quite be defined.

Worldly friendships sometimes have a hidden agenda. They may be politically or socially motivated, convenient arrangements that help one or both parties climb a ladder of success. Occasionally, friendships are based on neurotic needs: for example, perhaps one person likes to boss people around, and the other wants to abdicate any responsibility for his or her own life; so they have what might be called a symbiotic relationship (in which both are parasitic).

We sometimes call people friends who are merely frequently encountered acquaintances. These are people we see daily or weekly at work or church or bridge club—people whose first names and occupations we know but who aren't really important to our lives. They aren't quite in the category of friendship even though they are frequent occupants of our life space.

In this book I don't cover friendships within the family: husbands and wives who are best friends, parents who enjoy their grown children more than any other company, and so forth. I have an unusually close relationship with my children and could write another whole book on the subject, but because family relationships are in a special category of their own, this subject will have to wait.

An unsurpassing kind of friendship may be that which begins with friendship with Jesus Christ and extends to others who also love him. Such friends are a sign of healing to a brokenhearted world as they live out the phrase, attributed to Nero, "See how these Christians love one another!"

2

Friends in Christ

*Blest be the tie that binds
Our hearts in Christian love:
The fellowship of kindred minds
Is like to that above.
—John Fawcett, 1740–1817*

Some Christian friendships, just like any others, emerge out of common interests. Perhaps two people who sing in the choir enjoy each other's company and decide to meet for lunch together, or couples who work on the membership commission discover that they all like fly casting and so decide to spend a weekend angling for trout. Whatever mutual interest sparks them or however they begin, these friendships usually happen spontaneously.

Other Christian relationships are formed intentionally by two or more people for the sake of mutual aid and spiritual growth. These people may be impressed with one another's devotion to Christ or may believe that they could both benefit from praying together; they might make contact sporadically when the need arises or might meet regularly to pray or counsel or study. These relationships are often formed irrespective of any other basis for ordinary friendship. (For more about such relationships, see chapter 11.)

Whether built out of mutual interest or founded just for spiritual benefit, all true Christian friendships have some unique qualities because of Christ's example before the friends. The kind of love that Jesus offered from the cross transformed ordinary people and their relationships into a new kind of community; this transformation still goes on today in the Body of Christ.

True Christian friends try to *support* one another while building up the Church. They can remember, first of all, that Jesus died for them all, and this central fact can bridge the abyss of difference that human beings otherwise might find impossible to span. Despite opposing political persuasions, diverse backgrounds, or even strong denominational beliefs, Christians are given the gift of salvation that ties them together. This is the loving relationship that Scripture describes:

> If you have any encouragement from being united with Christ, if any comfort from his love, if any fellowship with the Spirit, if any tenderness and compassion, then make my joy complete by being like-minded, having the same love, being one in spirit and purpose" (Philippians 2:1-2).

Christian friends can also trust each other emotionally, treading lightly on fragile areas, trying especially hard not to push one another's "buttons." We know that we all have weaknesses and failings and tendencies to sin and that Jesus Christ treats us with tenderness and compassion. So we can be "like-minded," as the Phillipians passage suggests, and treat one another similarly. This kind of trust is especially important because it springs from the love of God, and when it is operative between two or more people, it helps to support the entire Body of Christ.

Trust is a product of openness and honesty on everyone's part. We won't have total emotional trust if we are "unequally yoked," either with someone who plays his or her cards too close to the chest, unable or unwilling to be exposed or vulnerable, or with someone who uses knowledge about us to dominate or hurt or manipulate. Christ does not want his Bride (the Church) to be a confused patchwork of anger and resentment and distrust. Perhaps this is why God's people have been warned so frequently in Scripture about mixing things. Exodus 23:19b instructs the Israelites not to cook meat and milk together; Exodus 34:25 reminds us not to mix a pure grain sacrifice with anything containing yeast; in Leviticus 19:19 Israel is told not to mate two kinds of animals, plant a field with two kinds of seeds, or to wear clothing made from two kinds of material. And more than a thousand years later, Paul warns Christians not to be "yoked" with unbelievers (2 Corinthians 6:14).

Another mark of Christians in a friendly relationship is the unique ability to confront one another occasionally without insult or anger or hidden motives. To say, "Jerry, I think you're feeling guilty about the insurance deal. Can't I help?" is not the same kind of inquiry that a worldly gossip, avid for power over others, uses to elicit information. Such concern is part of encouragement, one of the chief ministerial gifts of the church (see Romans 12:8).

Encouragement is an element that always seems to be present in Christian friendships. This sometimes comes in the form that all people, religious or otherwise, can understand: "Pat, I'm sure that you're going to be a wonderful teacher. You have a lot of skills to share, and your ability to deal with teenagers is a real gift." But another kind of encouragement is what the King James Version of the Bible calls "exhortation" in Scriptures such as 2 Corinthians 9:5; 1 Thessalonians 4:1, Titus 2:6; and Hebrews 3:13. This is the part of the leaven that lightens the Body of Christ through faithful encouragement to pray, to honor God, and to love and serve one another. Every Christian friendship has some level of exhortation going on in it, even if it's the mild remark, "Well, Mike, you've got a real problem here. Let's pray about it right now."

Encouragement sometimes doesn't feel too encouraging; in fact, it may be a downright irritant in your own life because the encourager may be asking you to do or see something in the light of Christ's love rather than in a way that seems "natural." On the other hand, I have heard some harsh words spoken under the guise of exhortation—the kinds of words that Christians must not say to one another because true encouragement always flows from love and will always be to God's glory in the end. Real encouragement will be accompanied by compassion and the encourager's own help; it comes as Paul's came to the Thessalonians: "You know that we dealt with each one of you . . . encouraging, comforting and urging you to live lives worthy of God, who calls you into [the] kingdom and glory (1 Thessalonians 2:11-12).

Perhaps the strongest mark of Christian friendship is that the relationship always brings the people closer to God. Whether they meet to taste foreign foods together, make lap robes for a retirement home together, or pray together, Christians will always have Jesus in their midst. The Church, as God plans it, is not a gathering of cliques, strung together like beads in a necklace. The Church is more like a tree, with each person or part necessary to the other. Friendship is an important part of the Body; therefore, Jesus is faithfully present in true Christian relationships, wooing the people in them to himself.

Unlike your somewhat guarded speech in places of business, in school, or in other secular places that you go in the course of a week, your conversation with a Christian friend can freely reveal your love for God. "I'll pray for your dad," "Thank God!" and "That reminds me of something I heard in last week's sermon," are the kinds of words that spring up naturally in Christian conversation, regardless of what the people are talking about. It takes only one Christian to be an instrument of God's peace; think how much greater a force several Christian friends can be! They will easily gravitate toward God in all they say and do.

Are you fit for Christian friendship? The "fellowship of kindred minds" is an ideal we all strive to achieve in our churches, in our marriages, and in our dearest friendships. There may be no greater pleasure than having someone reveal a kindred mind by nodding and saying, "Yes! You're exactly right!" or "Oh, I know what you mean!"

Some Christians have never had a problem making or keeping close friends. Others, although perhaps not always totally successful, are still happy and satisfied with their relationships. Then there are those who, by choice, have only a few close friends. These people are usually very busy, and when they do make friends, the relationships are for life. Sadly, however, the Church also contains those who never seem to make friends or those who can't keep the friendships that they enter. They have never known the Christian fellowship that's "like to that above."

Some of these people—perhaps even you—need a checkup, not to see if their hearts or lungs are in good shape, but to test their fitness for friendship. Insurance companies require physical checkups before they write most policies, and branches of the military put applicants through fairly exhaustive examinations. If you want to become a police officer or firefighter, you have to submit to a check of your physical and mental health as well as a check of your ability to perform some rigorous tests of strength and coordination.

But when you came into the fellowship of the Church, you were asked only to confess your faith in Jesus Christ (and in many denominations, to be baptized). You didn't have to submit a financial report or have your personality checked by a psychologist. Nobody had to know whether you had any money or gifts to contribute to the Body or whether you were even fit for the kingdom of God! Instead, you responded to Christ's message that anyone who wanted to do so might come, and you were received in that same spirit.

I frequently talk to "toddler Christians." They're half-grown, beyond the baby stage, but they're still not mature in the faith. Perhaps they've known Jesus long enough to settle down a little, but they are still learning and growing in the basics of the faith. They haven't lost their first love for Jesus; yet they often express a sad disappointment. Their disenchantment is not with the Lord or even with the worship and study of the church but with the fellowship they have found.

"One of the first things that attracted me to the Bentley Avenue church," said a new member, "was that the people seemed so friendly. But once I came forward to confess Jesus and was baptized, they seemed to forget about me and started working on someone else." I've heard such complaints more than once. This is a sad but occasionally accurate statement about some congregations who tend to put more emphasis on quantity than quality where church membership is concerned.

However, sometimes this statement comes from an "unfit" person who simply needs to work on the spirituality, social skills, temperamental development, or plain old love that it takes to be or make a friend. The skills of friendship need to be exercised every day if relationships are important to a person.

How do you know if you're in good shape for Christian friendship? Ask yourself the following questions:

1. Do I put the love of God before any human relationship? If it were just "Jesus and me," could I survive?

2. Do I keep my friendship with Jesus alive through constant dialogue with him, besides my daily prayer and study times?

3. Am I seeking a friend who has this same priority in his or her life?

4. Am I more attentive to my own spiritual and psychological flaws than I am to those shortcomings in other people?

5. Am I patient enough to let friendships grow slowly through their natural stages?

6. Do I have a personality interwoven with joy, compassion, hope, and realism?

7. Do I generously share my own gifts, and am I sensitive to the talents and gifts that others want to share as well?

8. Am I willing to look for friends among those who are of modest income and humble position in the community?

9. When people tell me something in confidence, can I be trusted absolutely to keep silent about it?

10. Do I understand that friendship is almost never exclusive, and am I willing to let my friend have other deep relationships without experiencing jealousy or hurt feelings?

11. Can I love the unlovable? Am I willing to be a friend to someone who doesn't want friends and to minister to someone who receives love arrogantly and without returning it?

12. Do I have trouble telling the difference between a friend and an Alligator? (If your answer to this one is yes, see chapter 7.)

If you answered yes to the first eleven questions, you are probably a good candidate not only for friendship but also for sainthood! Most of us can't give absolute answers to all these fitness-for-friendship questions; in fact, we may feel a little in the middle about some of them. However, if you can't honestly feel more positive than negative about most of the questions, perhaps you need exercise. Your friendship skills may be getting flabby.

Remember that fitness for Christian friendship is not measured by the world's standards. *First of all,* two Christians are really three because Jesus is always there with them. *Next,* remember that while the world preaches that we take care of "number one," meaning ourselves, those who love Jesus consider him Number One, the friend second, and self last. *Then,* remember that what the world considers weak and foolish is sometimes the very strength of a Christian relationship. Sometimes we even help our friends through our own failures!

For instance, I once had a neighbor who was downcast and unkempt; her mouth was full of whining and misery, and her three teenagers were just like her. They shouted and swore at one another through the filthy house, lied about everything, stole each other's money and possessions, and treated their mother as if she were an animal.

As much as I disliked their behavior, I was deeply concerned about this family, especially the mother; I could sense deep depression behind her loud complaints, her dull eyes, and her uncombed hair. As an experienced suicide preventer, I had some very real fears that she might try to kill herself. So I tried to keep the love that Jesus gave me flowing toward her, but I wasn't very successful.

Then came a time of very great difficulty for me. One of my grown daughters was critically ill; I was trying to care for her children and cook for her husband while I managed my own home and edited a Christian newspaper. To top off other problems we faced, my husband's company was on strike, and he had been home for ten months. We had run through our savings so that we were both anxious about money, and we were thrown together so much that we were getting on each other's nerves a bit. So one day I completely lost my temper.

I rarely get quite so angry, but on this day I even followed him out on the front porch, speaking in a very "spirited" voice, which someone else might call yelling.

After a little while, my neighbor rang the doorbell; when I opened it, she was holding a rose from the nearby florist's shop.

"You'll never know how much you've helped me today," she said.

"What?" I cried as I invited her inside.

"For the three years I've lived here, you always seemed to have it all together. Your house is clean, you're always happy and cheerful, you always look nice, and you have a career. Your grown kids seem to love coming over to see you. Your flowers bloom, and you even wash your car regularly. Who could live up to that? I was scared to death of you."

I choked back my impulse to interrupt and say, "You don't realize how many faults I have," and wondered if I should invite her into my office to show her what a mess I make when I work. But she went on.

"Today, when you stood on the front porch and yelled at your husband, I knew you were a human being. And I thought maybe we could really be friends!" She sat down and began to talk about her suicidal feelings for the first time.

In my weakness and foolishness I had helped this woman come close to me. It wasn't long before I was able to introduce her to Jesus and to watch him transform her life.

Whether you work through strengths or weaknesses or both, ask God to show you what you have to offer in the way of Christian friendship so that you can learn how to be a friend and how to be a Christian friend. This kind of prayer is a way you can "seek first the kingdom of God, and his righteousness" (Matthew 6:33; KJV)—first of all, by going to church for worship and devotion to God and second by acting lovingly toward others, even others who aren't necessarily birds of your own feather. Jesus said,

> If you love those who love you, what reward will you get? Are not even the tax collectors doing that? And if you greet only your brothers, what are you doing more than others? Do not even pagans do that? Be perfect, therefore, as your heavenly Father is perfect (Matthew 5:46-48).

3

Making Friends

As Jesus walked beside the Sea of Galilee, he saw Simon and his brother Andrew casting a net into the lake, for they were fishermen. "Come follow me," Jesus said, "and I will make you fishers of men." At once, they left their nets and followed him (Mark 1:16-18).

When Jesus called his disciples, there was something about him that was so irresistible and so dynamic that they knew he wasn't an ordinary person.

"Follow me," he said, and fishermen dropped their nets, tax collectors repaid those they had cheated, and women of shaky reputation turned pure as dawn. Jesus was the ultimate Friend, and all the people knew it when they saw him.

Most of us aren't quite so irresistible. We may have lips that drop Scripture like spring rain. Our hearts may be gentle and holy, and we may try to be attractive and good and loving in every way. But I still don't know anyone who could just say, "Follow me!" and have a parade of friends line up.

Therefore, we everyday people in the modern world form friendships a bit differently. These relationships most often meet a need in both people or rise out of a common interest; they are formed for mutual spiritual aid or because two people need each other's talents. Or maybe two people just happen to ride in the same car pool or have young children who also need friends and playmates. Probably the most frequent grounds for close friendship involve family relationships, church, work, or other interests like painting or jogging.

What happens when one is new to a city and doesn't have any common ground with anyone? Or how about a person whose life is solitary by default, such as someone who works in a one-person office or as a home-duty night nurse? What about a single mother with three preschoolers and a very limited budget or someone stuck alone in a warehouse doing inventory control?

About once a week, we can find a letter from one of these people in some newspaper advice column. The first axiom the "Dear Abbys" of the world give for making new friends is always "Go where there are people."

This suggestion is always good if you have plenty of time, your own transportation, and enough money; you might join a coin collector's club, take a night class in art appreciation, volunteer at the hospital, or work for a political candidate. But if you're looking for the special qualities that are found only in Christian friendships, you must look in the place where Christians congregate. This, of course, is the Church.

Churches don't have initiation fees, nor do they require that you have special skills to become part of their fellowship. The Church itself has, since its inception, considered friendship part of its fourfold ministry: Acts 2:42 tells us, "They devoted themselves to the apostles' teaching, and to the *fellowship [koinonia]*, to the breaking of bread and to prayer" (author's emphasis).

Make sure that you seek all four leaves of this biblical "clover." Going to church for fellowship alone may leave you with a vague feeling of dissatisfaction or even a sense of failure. Jesus wants his Bride, the Church, to be made of whole people who are willing to embrace the entirety of the faith.

Because the Holy Spirit is always nudging us to greater depth of this faith in Jesus, we won't ever be completely satisfied as "partial" Christians who want only the "apostles' teaching" through preaching or Bible study but who avoid fellowship; neither will we find fellowship sufficient without engaging in prayers and breaking bread in the Lord's Supper.

Go to church with an open heart and an accepting state of mind; go without any preformed ideas of the kinds of people you want to meet. Enter the church with your mind fixed, rather, on the personality of Jesus and his kingdom. If you go to church not looking for friends but looking for God, you'll find a whole community of companions and supporters. Make friends with Jesus, and "all the rest shall be added unto you."

If you absolutely have to work on Sunday morning, then go to a midweek evening prayer service or a Tuesday morning Bible study or whatever kind of service fits your requirements. Some cities even have come-as-you-are churches that you can attend in your most casual clothes! And if you are looking for friends, let it be known to the pastor or women's coordinator or youth group leader or adult Sunday school president that you'd like to be better acquainted with other members. And if you're new to the city or need friends, start looking around for your new church home.

I know you've heard someone—perhaps you yourself—say, "I went to such-and-such a church for six months, and although I loved the service (or the preacher or the choir), hardly anyone spoke to me." Perhaps the people in that church weren't sure that this slightly self-centered individual wanted to be spoken to; or maybe many of them were also shy or new to the church, waiting, as this complainer was, for someone else to start a conversation. I have also seen newcomers at church or other events look around quickly and scoot away before people had a chance to introduce themselves, much less strike up a conversation.

I grant you that some churches make friendships easier to form than others. Those with nametags and coffee hours and greeters and adult discussion groups are more helpful to strangers than those that have a lecture-style Sunday school and a service not followed by refreshments. I recently visited a church while I was on vacation, in which all visitors and newcomers were asked to use a blue coffee cup at the refreshment hour, so that others would be able to know for sure that here was someone new. But even in such churches the newcomer or the friend-seeker must occasionally take some responsibility for saying, "Hello. My name is [Mary Ann Smith or Alfred Jones], and I'm new here."

If you really want to have a Christian experience, pick another person who's standing alone. Try to zero in on someone who isn't your idea of a friend. Don't just be nice so the other person will like you; instead, try to meet his or her needs instead of your own.

For instance, if you're a young woman, you might talk to an elderly one and think about making her Sunday morning fuller while you're conversing. You might even invite her to go to a restaurant for breakfast with you after the service, if you have the time and money.

If you're a retired man, you could look around for a teenage boy whose mother has made him come to church. You'll be able to see his boredom and awkwardness on his face and in the way he stands during the coffee hour (probably against a back wall with his arms crossed). Find out what he does besides come to church—is he interested in sports or chess or nuclear disarmament or music? Listen to what he says and give him all the acceptance and approval and appreciation you can muster up.

"But you've said most of us tend to form friendships around what we have in common. Then why talk to people who are so different from us?" asks a reader.

First, you have a chance to minister to someone. Perhaps that youth may not be happy standing at the back of that room. You might have an opportunity to do God's work with a few pleasant words. Or maybe the elderly woman's children and grandchildren all live across the country, and she may be a recent widow. You can offer her your heart as a sign of God's love.

Second, that person may lead you to other friendships. For example, the teenage boy may have a dad or granddad or friend who fishes, makes puppets, bowls, goes sailing, or collects first editions, just as you do. Or maybe the teenager will mention you to the youth group leader, who is looking for an assistant. He can be a link in the chain of friendships.

Third, you may enjoy the very differences between you. My husband and I differ widely about almost everything. For instance, he works in the paperboard industry, surrounded by machines that chew up trees and make them into paper pulp; I, on the other hand, belong to a national conservation club, and I crusade against the pollution created by his industry!

When we go to a gathering, he likes to plow right into a crowd, greeting people, shaking hands and hugging all around, while I, not shy but much more reserved, tend to hang back a little, usually slipping into conversation with someone I know well; he thinks I'm a little cool, and I think he's brash. I like to swim every day, ride a bicycle, and camp; Ron likes to rough it in a good hotel. I could go on and on, but you can see the vast difference between our temperaments and interests. Yet we find that our differences are part of the peculiar mystery that makes us attractive to each other.

Last, no matter how different our ages or lifestyles may be, we all have something in common—or rather, Someone in common. We have a belief in the Lord Jesus Christ that is shared with the others we meet in the church, even if we're at a different spiritual level from some of them. Is your faith new, or have your experiences made it a little shaky right now? The church is full of others who are struggling, and they need to talk to people like themselves so that they don't think they're all alone (as you did). Are you a turned-on Christian with a burning desire to work for the Lord? You'll certainly meet your Christian counterparts in a congregation, and they'll be overjoyed to share their zeal with you.

What if you strike out the first time in trying to make a friend? What if the teenage boy is silent and embarrassed and doesn't want to talk? Or what if the widow loves your company but doesn't really lack for family and companions? Well, next Sunday or at the Wednesday night service, try again. First, speak to the teenager or the elderly widow again. Splash them with God's love. Then, speak to another "unlikely prospect." If you keep doing this every week, you'll suddenly discover one Sunday that you have a whole church full of friends and that every one of them has experienced God's love through you!

My husband is fond of saying, "Well, you could always do the most desperate thing first." Any time he says it, I know that he is reminding me to pray before I do anything at all. Therefore, before you seek friendship, you'll need to ask God to send others to you. Then follow your prayer with an act of faith, with a program of action.

"But shouldn't we just let God answer our prayers?" someone asks. Of course, but do what you can do, too, as an open sign of your faith in God's love. There are those who pray for help but ignore it when it arrives, not recognizing God's action right under their noses. They are like the man who sat on his roof, watching the flood rise and cover his house. Soon a friend came by in his boat and shouted for him to get in.

"No, thanks, I've decided to trust God to rescue me," he answered. His friend left, and he sat there awhile longer as the water rose. Then the county sheriff showed up in a speedboat.

"No, thanks," the man called. "I'm trusting the Lord." So the speedboat left.

The roof was nearly covered with water when a National Guard helicopter hovered down and offered him a rope ladder.

"No," he yelled, "I'm trusting God."

The helicopter left, the water rose until it covered him, and he drowned. When he got to heaven, he asked God, "Lord, why did you let me drown when I trusted you?"

"Let you drown? I sent two boats and a helicopter," God said. "What more did you want?"

Friend seekers may have boats and helicopters all around them, and yet they still wait for God's answer. If you're praying for friends, don't ever ignore anything in life—even the impossible—just because you don't see handwriting on the wall or hear a choir of angels!

4

Times and Speeds in Friendship

> *I trust in you, O LORD;*
> *I say, "You are my God."*
> *My times are in your hands. . . .*
> —Psalm 31:14-15

Time is a great factor in modern life, including the formation of most friendships. If you're getting to know someone better, perhaps at the stage of saying, "Say, let's get together for lunch," time has already entered your relationship. You'll notice it when you try to make a date.

If you're looking for friends, you need to decide beforehand what kind of time you have for friendship and how much time you have the right to ask for in return. Be realistic!

A woman who works in a busy medical office and goes home to a big house, three children, a husband, and two Labrador retrievers has less time for get-togethers than, say, an unemployed widow whose children are grown. A man who drives a long-haul truck route can't make the same kinds of commitments as his brother, who works as a real estate broker in a small city. A full-time student's time is so limited by classes and homework that he or she may have to find friends only at school with people who have the same schedules.

Whatever demands of time that families, jobs, and church make on you or your friend must be weighed against the value of a deepening relationship. After an honest assessment in early friendship, try to make your time schedules mesh, or offer to juggle some of your own commitments if you're really interested in getting together.

Be as giving as you can be and as understanding of another person's time as you can, without either of you feeling that you're making all the concessions. If your new friend is a young mother with two children in diapers, don't expect her to talk on the telephone for hours or to meet you for brunch; she's probably lucky if she can grab a piece of toast while she starts the wash. If you work during the day and also like to play tennis and you've met another tennis enthusiast who goes to work at midnight, think about playing at an indoor court some late evening. You may be a little tired at the end of your day, but isn't making a friend worth losing a few sets of tennis?

Sometimes time interferes so that a friendship that looks delightful can't quite bloom as it might otherwise. For instance, I keep rather strict writing hours (otherwise, I couldn't get a book like this written); so I don't have a great deal of free time. But sometimes, when my next-door neighbor or I long for companionship or we feel the need for exercise, we walk for a mile or two together. If it's lunchtime when we can get together, we might get on our bikes and ride up to the supermarket for a quick salad in the deli. Afterward, we both enthusiastically say, "Let's find a way to do this every day!" That doesn't seem to happen for either of us, since we're both working women; so we both have a rather wistful feeling about the friendship we're going to take time for, someday.

Obviously, we need to be reasonably flexible about our schedules, or we may miss even a taste of a really wonderful friendship. For instance, it's absolutely essential that a person have plenty of time alone with God, but a rigid time for prayer and Bible reading—one that can't ever be interrupted to see a friend who needs some companionship or help—should be reevaluated. If I never jumped up from writing a book about God to walk or bike with my neighbor, I wouldn't know her even as well as I do, would I?

Time can be either tyrannical or beneficent in Christian life. The first key to success in the battle for time is to remember that because of the commandment to love others, God will help us find time if and when we truly want to exercise that love in Christian friendship. The second key is to remember that we are *in* the world, not *of* it. We all have a full twenty-four hours every day, and we aren't supposed to get caught in secular systems or behave like people in a worldly rat race.

This is part of what Paul meant when he wrote, "Use the present opportunity to the full, for these are evil days" (Ephesians 5:16, NEB; instead of "use the present opportunity," the KJV says, "Redeeming the time").

Being realistic about your time for friendship also means accepting whatever another person's decision for himself or herself is. If you make friends with people who either seem so busy that your dates with them must always adhere to their strict schedules or are always late and never seem to get their appointments ordered, you have two choices: accept their rules for themselves, or forget the friendships! God sometimes sends people into our lives for counsel, and sometimes we can help them grow. But friends are another matter, and it is our privilege to defer to their schedules if we want to have a close relationship with them, even when they are either compulsive "worker ants" or irresponsible "grasshoppers."

Sometimes, God sets us straight about our own out-of-breath busyness, perhaps even convicting us of sin in this department. I know, because I most often have to battle arrogance—the kind of pride that manifests itself in workaholism. I love my work, and God has blessed it. But if I'm not careful, I can let the ambitions of the world, the arrogance of my flesh, and the snares of the "enemy" turn God's gift into a mountain of work.

For instance, I once told a publisher that I would finish a book in two months, even though very little of it had already been written. The publisher didn't ask me to do this but just asked for a completion date so that my contract could be drawn up.

To make things worse, the date I gave was just past Christmas! This meant that during the holidays I had to chain myself to my desk and miss a lot of music and celebration and fellowship with both friends and family. Was that really God's leading—or was it arrogance on my own part? I have a powerful feeling that I was just plain showing off how fast I could write. Or maybe I was so insecure that I thought the publisher's very generous contract offer would dissolve if I didn't hurry! Whatever the reason, time wasn't the tyrant—I was.

There is another kind of time that's very important in the formation and deepening of friendship. It's the natural timing of each individual life and personality, as it interacts with another life and personality in the steps of friendship.

Scientists are finding out that most of us are very sensitive to what they call "circadian rhythms." The term "circadian" comes from two Latin words that mean "about" and "day." In other words, my circadian rhythm is what my own biological and psychological timer thinks is a day. Perhaps this is the reason why we so frequently say, "Well, I guess I'll call it a day."

When these biological timekeepers are violated, as they frequently are for night workers who are really "day people" or airline pilots and diplomatic couriers whose travels "interrupt" normal time, the body and mind sometimes rebel by causing anxiety, depression, or physical illness.

Last spring, after two fast trips to New York and several out-of-town conferences that took place before I could get over my jet lag, I was seriously fatigued. I thought I might be getting the flu or worse; after a few more days, I feared that my mind was breaking down! Finally, I realized I was just out of step with my own inner drummer. It took several weeks of normal, quiet life—of eating properly, stuffing myself with vitamins, going to bed when I was tired and getting up when I was through sleeping—to get back to myself.

Moreover, the circadian rhythms are different for each of us; they are based on metabolism, morning blood pressure, and much else. For instance, my husband wakes up in the morning with what I consider to be a disgusting amount of enthusiasm. He would be perfectly happy to have long technical discussions at dawn. Once, as we lay in the dark of a January morning, listening to the gentle sound of the clock radio telling us that it was 6:02, his first words to me were, "Kris, do you know what you wrote check number 5561 for? It's blank in the check register." (Since I have very low morning blood pressure and wake up very slowly, my answer was just a soft whimper.)

On the other hand, I have a friend who gets out of bed at about ten A.M. but doesn't really come to life for twelve hours. She is sparkling and full of ideas at just about the time I go to bed, and she frequently even watches the sun rise and sleeps all that day.

I'm somewhere in between these two. I like to go to bed at eleven, read until midnight, and get up at around eight. I can do it differently, but that's the real me.

People have "other-people rhythms," too. These are the natural paces at which they relate to others. Each personality has its own basic speed of acquaintance and its own need for alone time. We can go against these rhythms, but it isn't usually wise.

Friendship has its own steps, which are a combination of our unspoken American "tribal ceremonies" and our natural, other-people rhythms. Sometimes, unfortunately, people either rush a new friend's rhythm or want to skip some steps.

Marie is just such a young Christian woman. Her eyes sparkle, and she almost dances when she walks. Her conversation is judiciously sprinkled with pleasant references to God's action in her life, and she is kind and loving to everyone she meets. But three or four times in her adult life, I've seen Marie in a state of grief because her hopes for a particular friendship did not materialize.

When Marie sees someone she'd really like to know better, she tries to take the friendship from zero to sixty miles per hour in about three weeks. She isn't realistic enough to understand that not everyone is as excited, creative, and instantly accepting as she is. She doesn't need time to know a person better, and so she rushes the process, not realizing that the person may need time to become better acquainted with her.

Of course, there are people who *never* want a real and deepening friendship; for more about these, see chapter 7, "How to Tell a Friend from an Alligator." But Marie isn't dealing with Alligators; she just runs ahead of most people, and it scares them.

The wish for instant intimacy is probably a product of our times. Those of us who lived through the sixties and seventies as adults may have been "encountered," "therapied," freed up, sensitized, and "seminared" on creative living until we almost expect to launch into a "meaningful relationship" with the person who puts gas in our cars.

I'm so used to this that I had a pleasant little shock several years ago. I wrote to an author about his book. It had moved me so much that I wanted to thank this very spiritual man. I was utterly charmed and astonished at the style of his reply:

> Dear Kristen,
> Forgive me for using your first name, but I love it, and besides, your wonderful letter overwhelmed me. . . .

I was deeply touched by this opening. I've been unblinkingly called by my first name by nurses in hospitals who were thirty years younger than I, by bank tellers, doctors, and editors the age of my youngest child; they seemed to have had no thought as to whether it was rushing our relationship (if, indeed, we had anything but a purely professional relationship).

Don't get me wrong: I'm glad the author and I broke down some barriers, and I certainly don't want any of my readers to think they have to write, "Dear Mrs. Ingram." But it was refreshing to note that a man of great spiritual maturity was at least aware that instant intimacy just isn't possible. Intimacy, depth of friendship, grows just as plants do. I can have an "instant" mature artificial plant—but if I want a real plant, I have to be patient and nurture it.

My friend Marie occasionally just barges into someone's life with a pure heart but with no grace. She can become absolutely obsessed with pushing a friendship, calling at all hours, offering too many small gifts, commenting on all the positive and negative aspects of her friend's personality and behavior. It's not just "I love your hair that way," but "I love to watch you eat because you have such a wonderful appetite," and "I am praying that God will help you become less of a perfectionist."

Eventually, there is always some kind of confrontation, with the potential friend asking Marie to back off and perhaps dropping the relationship altogether. Then Marie experiences terrible grief and depression.

"I only wanted to give her my love and friendship!" she cries. "Why did this happen?"

It happened because there are normal steps in friendship, and Marie wants to skip over most of them. She's good at the first one, so she wants to rush to the last immediately. Although every rule has exceptions and we are sometimes pushed by grace into a sudden, deep relationship with someone, the usual steps of making and keeping friends are the following.

1. First Acquaintance

You see someone at church, on the job, or at a club meeting, and you think, *That's my kind of person!* You may vow to reach out to him or her in friendship. Perhaps you smile at each other with compassion when a domineering Sunday school teacher gets particularly overbearing; maybe you both reach for the last oatmeal cookie when the dish is full of chocolate chip cookies. Whatever the mutual cause, whether it's a concern for getting rid of nuclear power plants or a shared love for split-leaf philodendrons, a certain feeling of camaraderie usually attracts us to most of our friends.

2. Reinforcement

You meet again either by chance or design. Maybe you went out for coffee after that first meeting, discovered that you had a lot in common, and made another appointment. If so, you're on your way faster than is average. Most people have several chance (or providential) "first acquaintance" meetings before they have the urge or the time to get to know each other better; and then it may be a chance comment or event that will make them talk to each other.

For instance, I had taught an adult Bible class at my church for a year when one Sunday morning I quickly sketched a rough drawing of the levitical priest in his ceremonial garb. Afterwards, one of the women asked if I were an artist, and I explained that I wasn't a real artist but had once been an elementary school art teacher. At this point her face lit up; she was currently teaching elementary school art! This was the beginning of a friendship that eventually grew beyond our shared interest in art.

3. Blessings, Bread, and Salt

In Arab countries one sign of friendship is for a person to sit down in another's tent, where they eat bread and salt together as a gesture of goodwill between them. Gestures of goodwill and bonding are found throughout history, up to the present day. People have exchanged beads, blessings, wallet photographs, blood oaths, or wampum to declare their peaceful intentions. (In ancient history, when war was over property and territory, everyone was a potential enemy. A person might steal another's goat or wife or settle on the other's land; so people made friends deliberately as a form of treaty.)

When I was in high school, some of us girls drove our mothers crazy when we exchanged small braids of our own hair with our best friends and wore each other's hair pinned over the new hole in our expensive perms. This is close to the ancient idea of exchanging blood in brotherhood, which made different people members of each other's body and tribe.

Most adults still exchange some kind of "wampum": they give out telephone numbers or business cards, and later, they have dinner at each other's homes or take turns treating each other to lunch. They display pictures of grandchildren or notice each other's Phi Beta Kappa key or compare allergy lists. Exchanging is an important part of the deeper reinforcement process, and several exchanges may take place.

Eating together is still the basic unit of exchange in friendship in most societies. It starts when people have coffee or a soft drink together and can culminate with dinner. There's something very primal about eating "bread and salt" together as a symbol of blessing, as a sign that the food is not poisoned and neither is the friendship!

4. Opening Up

At this phase, you may have been acquainted for a while as neighbors, members of a group, or co-workers. After one or more ceremonies of "Reinforcement" and "Blessings, Bread, and Salt" peculiar to your part of the country, you may be ready to express some personal feelings or thoughts.

Maybe you have lunch together one day to discuss the school carnival, and it lengthens into an exchange of inner feelings about rearing children and then about everything else. Or perhaps you almost break down during Bible study, and a class member stops you afterward to see what's wrong, listening compassionately while you sob out your problems with your mother-in-law or your employer. Or a casual golf buddy suddenly voices friendly admiration of your skill on the sixteenth hole (that's the par five with the pond in it) or expresses unusual appreciation for your sermon the past Sunday, and you end up calling your wives for a double dinner date to deepen the relationship between you as couples.

Whatever the circumstances, casual friends come to the place where they know and trust each other enough to exchange words, ideas, or feelings that are personal, thus deepening the relationship. This has to be done at the right speed and distance for both people. If it's too slow in coming, the friendship may remain a casual one; if it's too fast, one person may regret it and run away from such quick intimacy.

Sometimes God's love forces people in difficult circumstances past normal speeds into a closer relationship. When one of the women who lives on our cul-de-sac found that her husband had a month to live, I vowed that I would send at least one major food item to her home daily, so that she and the three grown sons who came from other cities could spend less time cooking for their barrage of callers and a little more time being with their loved one. Although we had never been more than casual friends who waved at each other, I got to know what a wonderful, strong, loving woman she is as I delivered food and picked up dishes and got medical reports. My neighbor and I came to know and love each other in a special way; by the time the terrible day came when her husband died, I felt very close to her and her family.

5. "Best" Friends

When someone becomes one's close or "best" friend, there is usually no special moment of recognition. In this society we don't celebrate the beginning of a deepening friendship the way we do an engagement to be married, the birth of a baby, or even the opening of a shopping mall!

But in some more "primitive" cultures, two people, usually men, may declare their eternal love and trust for one another. They each promise to protect the other's life in war or hunting and may be made a member of the other's family by an exchange of gifts, blood, or daughters (as wives).

In modern Western "civilization," however, where the enemy is not a wild animal or the member of another tribe but is more often our own psychological makeup, we don't declare this kind of friendship very often.

When we do, it is special. One of the treasures of my life is a note I received from an attractive, Spirit-filled woman who served with me on the staff of a weekend Christian workshop and was one of my dorm mates for the week-long event. We introduced ourselves in the parking lot; I helped her unload her car when she arrived. We discovered that we were both musicians, and I learned that she was a beginning writer. Of course, we talked into the night after each day's workshops. Her letter to me began, "Dear Kris: I really like you!"

When does casual friendship become deep friendship? There is not always one moment or event. What happens is a series of experiences that deepen your trust, affirm each of you as a worthy human being, and bind you to each other in Christian love. It may involve sharing difficult circumstances, as my experience with the neighbor whose husband was dying. Sometimes it happens when two people are in close proximity so that they go through all the first phases of friendship quickly, as my friend and I did at the workshop. Or the intimacy may simply grow over a long period until you find yourself saying, "Edward is my closest friend."

"Best" friends are not exclusive. They allow plenty of room for the other to work, live, and grow, and to have other friends. They are secure enough about each other's loyalty and affection not to let jealousy—a destructive emotion—be part of their relationship.

Close friends are honest, but *never* harsh or cruel. In the past two decades I've heard some awful things said in the name of "honesty," things that stripped other persons' defenses and damaged their egos. Good friends don't want to hurt each other or make themselves feel important at the other person's expense. So their candor is always couched in gentle terms. When someone says to me (usually rather proudly), "People tell me I'm very blunt," I find myself thinking of ways to get away from him or her. (I have a reputation for being rather outspoken myself, but you ought to hear what I *don't* say to my friends!)

On the other hand, it isn't necessary constantly to have what some call "charm." Worldly charm doesn't proceed from love; it is a mask, part of a sometimes necessary social structure that might belong in high-level international diplomacy, but not in close friendship. I'm talking about a kind of coquetry that covers up our real ideas, thoughts, or emotions. The blunt soul may be difficult, but he or she is a better friend than the "charmer" who makes me grip the arms of my chair as I wait for the axe to fall. "Charm" always makes me fearful of being manipulated.

True honesty is beautiful. Proverbs 24:26 says it delightfully: "An honest answer is like a kiss on the lips." Best friends are honest in this loving way—always salting candor with the remembrance that the other is someone Jesus died for.

6. Crossroads

At a certain point most of us in this upwardly mobile society move somewhere, unlike many of our grandparents who might have lived in the same house for sixty years. Ours may be a move across town to a different apartment, to the house we always wanted, or to the freedom of a retirement village; or it may be to another city, state, or country. Sometimes the move is a social or psychological one: one changes church denominations or has a crisis in faith; one suddenly decides to go back to school or join a country club that friends can't afford to join. Whether the move is physical or psychological, it puts the friendship at crossroads.

Most close friends who are separated manage to keep up with each other for a while. I know folks who are such admirable correspondents that they write regularly to scores of old friends, keeping the relationships alive with newsy letters. The efforts of others, more like myself, usually dwindle somewhat, and many of their past friends become memories and names on Christmas card lists.

Questions you aren't even conscious of may answer themselves when you are parted physically or vocationally from a friend. Do you still have a basis for relationship, or is it just habit? Is there really love between you, or is it sentiment for old times? You don't have to weigh these queries because often they'll work themselves out and you will drift into a sort of "back-burner" relationship.

But sometimes a friendship is so deep and so dear that you may want to continue to call each other "best friends," even though you aren't together very often. I met my friend Shirley, to whom this book is dedicated, in the ninth grade. We went to the same school and belonged to the same church youth group; we both loved our French teacher, Miss Goodrich, and hated geometry and a girl who rode on the bus with us. Sometimes we even liked the same boy, which occasionally created problems, but our friendship weathered the storms. Shirley was baptismal sponsor of Susan, my first child, now grown, and she has never forgotten Susan at Christmas, birthday, or graduation, even after her duties as godmother were finished.

Our lives have changed, of course, and we pursue our own separate aims and dreams. Our incomes are considerably different, and we share few hobbies. Shirley does exquisite needlework, of museum quality, and she is knowledgeable about the history of folk arts such as Bayeux tapestry. While I admire her work and knowledge, most of my interests run in another direction. She had her children later than I did, so that she was still mothering long after I was completely free from buttoning sweaters and wiping noses. We're both terrible correspondents, finally calling each other in the throes of long-distance guilt. Our religious lives seem to be spaced farther than our thousand-mile geographic difference.

But when we're together, we pick up exactly where we left off, understanding each other perfectly and without criticism, admiring, sharing, and expressing our fondness easily.

Many of you will say that you, too, have a friend in this category. How do such friendships go on? How can Shirley and I, who live so far apart and are so different, continue to be sure of each other's affection and loyalty? This is possible when people are, first, willing to give generously of their time, and, second, willing to recognize each other's pace. We took our friendship one inevitable step at a time and somehow nurtured and reinforced it; we exchanged blessings, lived through trauma, and determined that, no matter what, we would love each other. Now our loving, caring friendship is one of the treasured facts of our lives.

Time is man-made; God lives *outside* time, looking at the beginning and the end, the Alpha and the Omega, seeing at once the first and last seconds of human existence. And the tyranny of time is also humanly manufactured, especially when time begins to rule (and perhaps ruin) a fact of friendship.

I have talked to many unhappy people whose spouses were full-time workaholics—ambitious executives who scarcely ever came home and persons who spent more time cleaning house and cooking than they did being with the lonely partner. We all need to reevaluate constantly the amount of time we think we have against how much time we need to do the things we want to do.

If every minute is crammed full, maybe you've got a bad

case of pride; if your other-people rhythm never seems to relax for a new friend, maybe you need to pray for a flesh-and-blood heart!

Is there someone in your life who is making overtures of friendship? If someone is on the hem of your garment right now, is there really no time or space in your life for another friend? Really?

5

The Taming of the Tongue

If anyone considers himself religious and yet does not keep a tight rein on his tongue, he deceives himself and his religion is worthless (James 1:26).

Some Pharisees and lawyers came to Jesus and asked, "Why do your disciples break the tradition of the elders? They don't even wash their hands before eating!"

Jesus reminded them of their own hypocrisy in keeping the Law; then he called to the crowd and said, "Listen, and understand with your hearts. What goes into people's mouths doesn't make them 'unclean'; but what comes out of their mouths, that's what makes them 'unclean'" (see Matthew 15:1-2, 10-11).

Throughout his ministry, Jesus suggested that words—and the thoughts that produce them—are powerful. He told the Pharisees that on the day of judgment they would have to account for every careless word they had ever spoken; in fact, the words themselves would acquit or condemn them (Matthew 12:36-37).

In the wilderness Jesus reminded the Tempter that the very sustenance of being is not in the creation of grain for us to eat, but in God's speaking (Matthew 4:4; Deuteronomy 8:3). And in his wonderful high priestly prayer on the night of his arrest, Jesus said that God's Word is the truth in which believers are sanctified (John 17:17).

In Jesus' words and the writings of his apostles, we find a consistent theme: Two facts about words are important in all Christian relationships. The first is that God's Word, sown in the good soil of our hearts and minds, can produce thirty- or sixty- or a hundredfold within us (Mark 4:3-8). The second is that the spoken word—perhaps the offhand remarks we make to friends and families and co-workers—can even give life or destroy it (John 6:63;68).

Think of the hurts you have sustained in your life and the hurts that you no doubt regret having inflicted on others. Haven't most of these injuries been caused by words? Now think of the moments of your greatest joy, and you will undoubtedly find that spoken words are at the source of such happiness, too. Words can be the most powerful force in human life, for when you speak, you imitate God, who spoke the word that created the universe.

Following are ten great principles for making speech fit for the holy ground of human friendship, along with some exercises to improve them as skills.

1. Remember that you are always in God's presence.

Would you stand in front of God's throne and yell at your neighbor about his dog, snarl at a waitress who was slow, or quarrel spitefully with your teenagers about the car? Well, remember that if you ever do these things, you do them in front of God, because we are always before the throne. In fact, the reason many devout Jewish men wear a head covering at all times is that a male Jew never speaks of God or to God with a bare head; and when are God and prayer not part of our daily, hourly life and speech and work? (Some Jews even wear their prayer shawls all day.)

Perhaps we all need something to remind ourselves that God is present and that our lives move in that Presence. Most of the time we are unconscious of that fact, just as a fish may not realize that it lives in water. We sometimes tend to think of God as "out there" rather than "in here, now."

It would seem fitting, then, to make conversation with friends a throne-room experience for both of you, using the kinds of words that you want God to use in speaking to you—words of acceptance and mercy.

"Speak and act as those who are going to be judged by the law . . . because judgment without mercy will be shown to anyone who has not been merciful. Mercy triumphs over judgment!" (James 2:12-13). The more you acknowledge God's listening presence in and through and around you, the more reverent and careful you will be in speech to others. Soon showing love in your words will become a lifetime habit.

Exercise: Increase your awareness of God's presence by spending five minutes each morning in the devout silence of personal worship, comparing that Presence to the air around you. Feel God enveloping your body, your room, and your house. Visualize a close friend, also in the "envelope" of God's presence. During the day, constantly "devote yourself to prayer, being watchful and thankful" (Colossians 4:2).

2. "Let the word of Christ dwell in you richly . . ." (Colossians 3:16).

Having Christ's word dwelling in you richly so that your whole personality is flooded with it doesn't mean just reading and memorizing a lot of Scripture. Even the Pharisees were loaded with verses from the Bible, and tradition says that Satan can quote with the best of us!

Remember that Jesus is the Word who came to live on earth with us, and that he longs to be your constant Companion, Brother, and Friend. If your heart is a throne for Jesus, the rest of you—body, mind, emotions, and spirit—will be deeply affected and the words that you speak can be valuable in bringing the world into Christ's kingdom life.

Call constantly on the Holy Spirit to inspire you about Scripture. It wouldn't do any good to memorize the whole Bible unless you had the Holy Spirit's help in understanding and using this knowledge. And when you do memorize a passage from the Bible, do it for God; let it be used for your own edification and not just to prove a point to someone or manipulate other people!

Exercise: Read John 15:1-17 every morning for a week. (If possible, use several different translations to get the feeling of the Word, not just the words.) Each day write a line or two about what the Scripture means to you, and follow with a prayer that the Holy Spirit will "guide you in all truth."

3. Speak to other people with love and reverence, as to Christ.

Jesus told his followers that whatever we do for others, we do for him (Matthew 25:31-46). Martin Buber, the great Jewish theologian, suggests that we experience God, in what he has so magnificently called "I-Thou," only when we are in dialogue with God's other children:

> The moments of relation are here, and only here, bound together by means of the element of the speech in which they are immersed. Here what confronts us has blossomed into the full reality of the Thou. Here alone, then, [is] reality that cannot be lost. . . .[1]

James, who had the same manner of hitting the nail on the head as Jesus, said,

> With the tongue we praise our Lord . . . and with it we curse men, who have been made in God's likeness. Out of the same mouth come praise and cursing. . . . Can both fresh water and salt water flow from the same spring? (James 3:9-11).

Of course, you know that a spring can't give salt and fresh water. But do you (for instance) sometimes leave an early-morning Bible study and go to work—and then later become so annoyed with people's stupidity on the job that you "tell them off" or seethe with wrath? Or do you occasionally become so angry with traffic on your way to church on Sunday that you call other drivers idiots (or worse) and then feel unfit to enter the church and praise God?

There are those who justify themselves when they discover they're angry by pointing out that a co-worker or another driver did something dangerous or foolish. But Scripture doesn't differentiate between real fools and those who annoy us; it simply says that if we say to any other person, "You fool!" we are "in danger of the fire of hell" (Matthew 5:22).

Exercise: One of the sweetest Christian exercises is to pretend (or to remember!) that the person we are talking to is Jesus and that every word we say to that person is said to our Lord. Each day pick out a family member, co-worker, or neighbor and converse with that person, pretending that he or she is actually Jesus in disguise.

---

[1] Martin Buber, *On the Bible: Eighteen Studies*, Nahum N. Glatzer, ed. (New York: Schocken Books, Inc., 1968), p. 15; quoted by Stephen M. Panko in *Martin Buber* (Waco, Tex.: Word, Inc., 1976), p. 65.

4. Speak about other people with the same reverence and love you use in speaking to them.

Don't carry tales whether they are true or untrue. Even if you are careful not to judge a person's behavior, you're just as guilty if you report that behavior to someone else who *will* judge it. And be careful that what you say about others isn't gossip disguised as "Christian concern." I have been to some prayer meetings at which the prayer requests came in the form of some pretty juicy information. When you see someone doing something self-destructive, go to the person, not to others, if you have to talk about it; and when you visit a person who is doing something you consider sinful, make sure you go as a friend, not as a judge. If you request prayer for someone, give the first name and a brief description—such as, "Willie needs prayers about a family problem." God knows the details; no one else need know.

Slanderous and judgmental gossip can destroy more than friendships; it has wrecked marriages and driven its victims into deep depression. It is a tool used by those ambitious and envious souls who feel the need to be important, and they deliver their plums of information with some triumph.

I know a man who "ran down" his wife—to whom he was pledged, by marriage vows, as best friend—not only to his cronies but to her relatives and their mutual friends; he even called on her women friends when she was out of town and presented himself as "misunderstood." His gossip, rooted in his own feelings of blue-collar inferiority to his professional wife, backfired; every word he ever spoke against his wife was taken back to her. Soon he had no friends at all, and she found it difficult to trust him after that.

If that man had been better grounded in Scripture, he would have remembered what James told us:

> . . . Do not slander one another. Anyone who speaks out against his brother or judges him, speaks against the law and judges it. When you judge the law, you are not keeping it, but sitting in judgment upon it. There is only one Lawgiver and Judge, the one who is able to save and destroy. But you—who are you to judge your neighbor? (James 4:11).

Exercise: Every day for a week read Psalm 15. At the end of that time, go outdoors or to a plant store and get about ten smooth stones. On these stones, write any infraction of God's law that you have ever committed. If the stones are all blank, ask some friends to help you throw them at the first sinner you see. (See John 7:53—8:11, the story of the woman taken in adultery.)

5. If someone tells you something in confidence, handle that trust with care.

When your friend tells you something and asks that it not go beyond that room, you have been given one of the great gifts that friendship contains: trust. Ask God to help you forget, immediately, what the friend has told you. If you think you won't be able to keep a confidence, say to your friend, "I love you too much to take a chance with this. Don't tell me," or "I don't keep secrets from my spouse. If that isn't all right, then maybe you shouldn't tell me."

If you do betray a confidence, either because you accidentally dropped information or names or because you just couldn't keep it, go immediately to your friend and confess before he or she finds out from someone else. You are more likely to save the friendship this way. Besides, you owe a confession of your faults to those whose confidence you have betrayed (see Proverbs 28:13). And who knows? Perhaps your friend, who offered you the gift of trust, will now offer you the greater gift of forgiveness.

Exercise: People who feel trust toward others are usually trustworthy themselves; so this activity is designed to help you trust others—including God. On several small slips of paper, write something about yourself that you don't want advertised. This might be something negative about yourself, or just a nice secret that isn't for publication yet. Put the slips of paper into an envelope; then seal it and give it to a friend—even a rather casual friend, if you really need to learn to trust and be trusted. Ask that person to return the envelope to you, still sealed, in a month. When it is returned, thank your friend for being trustworthy; if possible, pray together and thank God for being the One who teaches us to love one another through keeping confidences.

6. Bring a positive energy into your environment.

There's nothing worse than having a Pollyanna around, preaching sweetness and light when our lives are in crisis; even small discomforts are not lightened by these platitude speakers. I think the closest I ever came to murdering another human being was when I broke a large glass container of olive oil on the kitchen floor while my youngest child was in his playpen, screaming for lunch. To top it off, my cat began climbing the doorscreen and crying, while the dog barked furiously. I was feeling rather testy as I slipped and picked my way through broken glass in a sea of oil, looking for the mop and maybe someone to blame and wondering if my child would starve before I could get across the room to feed him. At that point, a visiting neighbor, lounging at the dining table (well out of the spill area) shook her finger playfully and said, "Now, Kris, just praise the Lord for this oil mess. Remember, all things work together for good, dear!"

Nobody needs this kind of "positive thinking," especially from someone who doesn't seem inclined to offer any help beyond words. On the other hand, a loving word can be infinitely helpful; as Scripture says, "Pleasant words are a honeycomb, sweet to the soul and healing to the bones" (Proverbs 16:24). Mercy and loving-kindness are worth more than gold to our broken and suffering world; those who study such things have discovered that sinful people grow better when they are encouraged and given positive reinforcement than when they are negatively confronted.

A "pleasant word" doesn't mean saying, "Cheer up!" or "Think of those who are worse off." It means offering an attitude of encouragement, giving the friend acceptance and a reason to look forward to your coming, with words like, "I understand." It may even mean the phrase that is hardest to say: "I'll help you!"

Exercise: Spend three days without saying anything negative or discouraging to any others or anything depressing or self-pitying about yourself. These days may seem long and difficult, but they offer rich rewards. When you have completed those three days, take a deep breath—and do it for three more! Keep going until this is a habit.

7. Spend more time listening than talking.

The epistle of James reminds us to "take note of this: Everyone should be quick to listen, slow to speak . . ." (James 1:19).

Those of us who are lucky enough to have a longtime close friend nearly always say something like, "She [or he] understands me." That means that our friends are people who have been listening to us, because people understand us best when they are listening to us. It probably also means that you, too, have listened creatively, because the conversation of friendship is always reciprocal.

People have made job decisions, worked out marital problems, and even been prevented from suicide by the creative listening of good friends. I suspect that one reason so many people end up in psychotherapy is that we have lost the art of listening to our friends; only the paid therapist seems to offer that kind of response. One of the values of Christian friendship, then, is to be quick to listen so that the friend can rely on our compassion and comprehension.

Exercise: Creative listening does not mean sitting in absolute silence while another holds a monologue, nor does it mean merely waiting for your turn to talk. Start being (not just pretending to be) interested in what another person is saying, accepting what the other says even when you don't particularly like what you're hearing. Include asking questions, saying, "Tell me more," and occasionally using a clarifying phrase such as "I think I hear you saying. . . . Is that what you meant?" Try these techniques for at least a week with everyone you talk to. By then you will probably have several new friends!

8. Learn to react with love, not anger, to what others say.

James continued his advice about being quick to listen and slow to speak by saying, ". . . and [be] slow to become angry, for . . . anger does not bring about the righteous life that God desires. Therefore get rid of all moral filth and the evil that is so prevalent, and humbly accept the word planted in you, which can save you" (James 1:19-21).

Christians have no business being touchy or huffy about what others say or do or trying to think up "smart" or vengeful answers, regardless of others' behavior. It may be hard for Christians to think of themselves in terms of the "moral filth" that James was talking about since they rarely indulge in obscenity or perversion or other activity that might be thought of in these terms. But hurt feelings, when they are a mask for anger and wounded vanity can be sins—because they may be behaviors that are rooted in pride, which is perhaps the greatest of all sins!

James used the phrase "the evil that is so prevalent." What

is being bandied about in our society may, indeed, be a prevalent evil—ideas like standing up for our rights or defending ourselves or evening the score. Peter reminds us that Jesus, when he was insulted, "did not retaliate; when he suffered, he made no threats. Instead, he entrusted himself to him who judges justly" (1 Peter 2:23). If you feel insulted, pray about it and, trusting God to take care of the matter, put it out of your mind.

Exercise: If you find yourself operating in the "touchy" mode, spend some time alone in prayer and find out what's at the bottom of it. Read the passages of Christ's arrest and Passion in the four Gospels and notice how he responded even to those who persecuted him. Write down the names of all people who currently upset you; then ask God to forgive them and to help you forgive them.

Sometimes such anger comes from old rage at our parents or some other persons. Pray that these people be forgiven for anything they did to mistreat you, and then ask God to forgive you for nursing a grudge. You may find it difficult to face some of your own buried anger; if this is the case, seek some counseling from your pastor or a Christian counselor on getting rid of old rage.

9. Always speak with humility and courage, and give equal favor to all persons, irrespective of their social status.

Are you ever tempted to be ambitious or to boast? Think of the consequences: you might end up guilty of pride (or at least guilty of becoming a famous bore)! We're often encouraged by the world's standards to envy and strive against each other; even Christians sometimes do it, but they like to call it "healthy competition"! Scripture warns us, over and over, to be humble, to abandon worldly ambition, to pile up treasure in heaven instead of on earth. But a present-day trend suggests that God really wants us to be rich and important.

We are rich—but only if our treasure is Christ. We are important—if our names are written in the Book of Life. All the rest of the world's goods and temporal power are transitory; for some of us who have a tendency to become envious or to covet another's wealth or position, such goods can become the objects of sin.

Consider the boaster. We've all been stuck, at least once, with a braggart whose conversation is nothing more than a list of his or her accomplishments, goals, talents, influential friends, and opinions about everything. These people run roughshod over gentler types, and since their whole goal is to impress us or to curry the favor of those people they deem important, they aren't interested in the interchange of true friendship. They have forgotten that love is patient and kind, doesn't boast, and isn't proud (see 1 Corinthians 13:4).

Then there are the pompous, the officious, the name droppers, and the self-important, who bustle about doing their jobs as if the means were more important than the end. Children in this category become bullies when they are hall monitors; adults do the same thing, perhaps in a more subtle way.

Braggarts and pompous people and name droppers are, of course, really insecure. They lack self-esteem, and substitute self-importance for it. This insecurity robs them of the possibility of courage; they seem to need important friends or a powerful position to feel important. It takes real fortitude to face ourselves as we really are, to appraise our own sinfulness honestly—a fortitude they don't seem to use.

This kind of behavior is prideful, underhanded, and self-serving and not in line with Scripture: ". . . as believers in our glorious Lord Jesus Christ, don't show favoritism. . . . If you show special attention . . . have you not discriminated among yourselves and become judges with evil thoughts? . . . If you show favoritism, you sin and are convicted by the law as lawbreakers" (James 2:1-4,9). "Such 'wisdom' does not come down from heaven but is earthly, unspiritual, of the devil. For where you have envy and selfish ambition, there you find disorder and every evil practice" (3:15-16). "As it is, you boast and brag. All such boasting is evil" (4:16). "Therefore confess your sins to each other and pray for each other so that you may be healed" (5:16).

Exercise: I'm sure, of course, that none of you is ever boastful or envious or pompous. But just in case you see an unpleasant tendency in yourself, try this: Volunteer for a month to wash people's feet in a nursing home or convalescent home, and don't tell anyone else you're doing it. During this time, refrain from offering your usual gifts (playing the piano, speaking, decorating the parish hall, running a meeting, etc.) anywhere; thank God daily for the service you can offer your brothers and sisters in the home. Every evening before going to bed, read John 13:1-17. And for the rest of your life, if you must boast, let it be of Christ! (See 1 Corinthians 1:31; 2 Corinthians 10:17; Galatians 6:14.)

10. "Be wise in the way you act toward outsiders; make the most of every opportunity. Let your conversation be always full of grace, seasoned with salt, so that you may know how to answer everyone" (Colossians 4:5-6).

The charge to "make the most of every opportunity" seems to inspire some well-meaning but unseasoned Christians to pin down their acquaintances with a set of spiritual principles and demand a commitment to Christ on the spot. Or they may accost strangers on buses, on airplanes, or in shopping malls, present them with a handful of tracts, and cheerfully demand, "Are you saved?"

Paul's message to the church at Colossae suggests that this is not usually the best way to go. Conversations that are "wise, full of grace, and seasoned with salt" show we are interested enough in other persons to know something about them and about what they already believe and to offer them loving friendship before we ever offer them the plan of salvation. In fact, Paul says that "you are to be ready to answer everyone," suggesting that we let our friends be so attracted to our grace-filled lives that they are impelled to ask about Jesus!

Know what you are talking about. More harm has been done to Christ's church through ignorance than through heresy! Don't assume that the atheist who lives across the street is evil and not worth your time; true atheists or honest agnostics are usually thoughtful, ethical people. Likewise, don't assume that every other church but yours is an apostate religion. Calling your friend's religion a cult can be dangerous, too. One time at a prayer workshop I met a woman who announced that Judaism was a cult. She attempted to prove the point by saying that Jesus used "another book" instead of the Bible. She meant the Torah, not knowing that she was talking about the first five books of the Old Testament. Another woman, who belonged to a Christian sect that believes itself to be the only true religion, recently tried to hire a cult deprogrammer to rescue her son—from another main-line Christian denomination!

If you have a friend whose religious life is rooted in a non-

Christian faith, find out something about it before you bumble ahead; your knowledge may truly pay off. Let me give you an example. I knew a young woman, a friend of my daughter, who was reared as a sort of "haphazard" Protestant but whose family never really located itself in a church. In her twenties she became interested in a sect of Buddhism which she thought met all her needs. Neither my daughter nor I had tried to talk to her about Jesus but she must have sensed something spiritual in the atmosphere because she was always drawing one of us into a conversation that compared Christianity and Buddhism.

Dealing with this comparison was easy for me. I had studied comparative religion at length, having grown interested in the workings of Buddhism when I was investigating Oriental art. I had also read a good deal of Buddhist literature, much of which, I told her, I admired for its piety and discipline.

"Then what do you have that I don't have?" she asked rather defiantly.

"I don't have to stand Karma, as you do. Someone did that for me," I answered, trying to keep my voice casual, as her mouth fell open. I had spoken, in her own religion's language, about Christ's atoning work on earth. I had reminded her that Karma—the law of cause and effect that mercilessly demands the correction of past-life mistakes and the payment for past-life sins in succeeding incarnations—could not affect my life even if I did believe it existed (which I don't). Jesus had taken the punishment for my sins, or "Karma," upon himself. I didn't call her belief in reincarnation nonsense; I just calmly showed her where she was and where she could be.

"Tell me about it!" she said, her eyes shining. And I did.

Seasoning your conversation with salt means making it flavorful and good-tasting. I think that a conversation seasoned with salt would be one without "proof texts." It's important to consider every verse of Scripture in the context of every *other* verse of Scripture so that we can give God's whole message, not just a few texts, to the world. And let your friends see how peaceful and satisfied you are in your life with Jesus, while you continue acting like a wise and sensible man or woman instead of being a person who makes friends just to add to the number of convert notches you can put in your belt. People who do the latter tend to create opportunities for themselves rather than make the most of those that God sends.

On the other hand, Paul does ask us to be ready to answer everyone; and Jesus sends us, just as God sent him (John 20:21). Therefore, be immersed in prayer and Scripture, so that when your opportunity does come to sow or to reap, you will be ready.

Exercise: Without quoting from the Bible, write down your own thoughts, in your own words, in answer to these commonly asked questions:

1. If God is all-powerful and all-loving, why does evil exist in the world? (Evil in this sense refers to suffering, sickness, children born with cancer, good and innocent people killed by tornados, etc.)

2. How could God become a man on earth and still be in heaven?

3. Does God throw a righteous Buddhist, for instance, into hell with someone like Hitler? And if Hitler believed in Jesus, did that keep him out of hell while the good Buddhist had to go there?

4. Does God really run everything? Is God in charge of an airplane so that it doesn't crash? Then what happens when one does go down—does God make that happen, too?

5. If God created everything, who created God?

These are just a few of the serious questions that people ask about the Christian concept of God. They may sound simple, even foolish—but they aren't easy to answer! After you have answered them in your own way, read some Scripture to help you understand whether your own answers are sound (such as Job 38; Psalm 77; Isaiah 40; John 1:1-18; Romans 14:1; Ephesians 2; Hebrews 1:1-4; 1 Peter 3:18-22; and 1 John 2:1-2). If possible, read the works of some modern Christian apologists like C. S. Lewis or A. W. Tozer.

Is your tongue tamed? Wonderful! Is it still a little unruly? That's wonderful, too, because it means you have something else to pray about, that will keep your fellowship with Christ active, and fellowship with Jesus is always a transforming experience.

6

Healthy Self-Esteem—And Myths About Self-Love

*Just as I am, without one plea,
But that thy blood was shed for me.*
—Charlotte Elliott, 1789–1871

There are millions of miserable people in our society who are so disabled emotionally that they can't be friends to themselves or anyone else. These are often people who as children had their ideas viciously ridiculed or their actions constantly directed and unmercifully criticized. Many also have been physically or sexually abused as children. There are people who were traumatized by terrible, unusual experiences, like those who grew up in Nazi concentration camps in the shadow of the Holocaust. Still others have been brutalized by a spouse or other close person until their self-image is ugly and distorted.

Though he or she may have Christ as Savior, such a victim is not always instantly healed when he or she is baptized. These emotionally needy people definitely need to be built up into Christian wholeness. Friends can lovingly, generously help to make up for the unjust, unloving treatment given them by those who should have loved them more. Friends can also help to break the vicious pattern that can lock such people into a lifetime of despair; otherwise, those who are traumatized may be likely to enter unconsciously into similar relationships when they are adults. Unless the pattern changes, their friendships and marriages may be based on what they fear most—rejection and abuse!

Individuals who are badly scarred by life may have serious or fatal "accidents" at home or in traffic; often they openly attempt (and some succeed at) suicide because they loathe themselves or feel terribly inadequate. They are usually convinced (with help from their abusers) that the physical battering and rejection they experience are somehow their own fault, even believing that the abuse and feelings of rejection are "signs" that they are unworthy to live.

This terrible cycle can be interrupted by counseling and support-group interaction, but it needs to be recognized and treated in the professional friendship of psychotherapy. These people need the security of the special relationship found in intensive counseling in order to gain normal self-esteem.

People who need help to become better friends to themselves probably fall into one of these categories:

> Those who are always or nearly always bored, restless, or unhappy unless they're with other people. "Isn't wanting to be with others a healthy sign?" you may ask. Yes, but not if one can't be happy alone! People who have an optimum amount of self-esteem always need to have some time alone to pray, think, and work. Jesus often went off by himself to pray and think during his ministry, because solitude is necessary for deep communion with God as well as for emotional restoration. People who cannot be alone lack the ability to be whole, to be complete persons, without dependence on someone else taking care of them. The desire for love is translated into insatiable need. Such persons aren't centered enough in their own lives or in the personhood of Jesus to be responsible for their own feelings and to rest in the joy of the Lord.

> Those who have been emotionally deprived, abandoned by parents, married to cold, unsympathetic spouses, or reared in emotionless families. They need (and sometimes even demand) constant reassurance and affirmation. If they give a gift or do a favor, they fish for more and more thanks and

recognition of the gift's appropriateness. They ask for approval and acceptance and appreciation all the time and even feel cheated if others don't notice or mention their appearance or other qualities.

Those who talk about themselves, their emotional and physical problems, their bad childhoods or painful marriage experiences more than any other subject. Such people tend to dominate conversations. Often, they are trapped in the belief that these admittedly terrible experiences of physical, mental, or sexual abuse by parents, spouses, or other persons who were (or are) significant in their lives are completely responsible for all their present actions and personalities.

Occasionally, one of these scarred individuals may already have had so much therapy, counseling, and inner healing that he or she thinks every relationship is a therapeutic one and that the only way of "sharing" is to go over and over and over the terrible life experiences, not realizing that in doing so he or she is still holding onto grief instead of being healed.

Unhappy self-centeredness is sometimes called "negative narcissism," and if this is your problem, I would suggest that unless you have had (or are having) extensive counseling or "healing of the memories," you might want to investigate some inner healing techniques. An excellent book to read is *Healing Life's Hurts,* by Dennis and Matthew Linn.[1] You may also get some help from attending a meeting of an organization like Al-Anon. Although this group was formed to aid the friends and families of alcohol abusers, its philosophy can get people on the right track by helping them drop their "victim" mentality and become responsible for their own present lives.

But there's another kind of neediness that should be present in *all* of us. It doesn't come just from emotional sources. It is in the recognition of our own need that we find Christ. As Catherine Marshall wrote, "If you are satisfied with your life

[1] Dennis Linn and Matthew Linn, *Healing Life's Hurts* (New York: Paulist Press, 1978).

and feel no need for any help outside yourself, this book is not for you. The search for God begins at the point of need."[2]

Now that we have looked at the damaged ego, we need to look at the other side of the self-love coin. Although the symptoms that arise from emotional crippling are detrimental to Christian friendship and life in general, the alternative is not necessarily to rush into a love affair with ourselves! Those of us who have wearily survived the "Me" decades may need to take a look at some ideas about ego that are prevalent in our society. What are the current myths about self-love? How do they affect friendships? And how does the Bible stand in contrast to the world's standards?

Myth: Jesus told us that we are supposed to love ourselves in order to love others.

Anyone who has been alive and literate in this century has read or heard, perhaps more than once, that Jesus' instructions to love one's neighbor as oneself (Luke 10:27) were given to us as a call for self-love. I have even heard this interpretation from Bible teachers and pastors. But Luke 10:27 was not intended as a lesson in self-esteem; Jesus was talking about having friendship with God and being decent to other people.

Read the entire passage in Luke 10:25-37. It began with a Pharisee who wanted to test Jesus—perhaps even trick him into making a heretical remark. Jesus responded with what we call the "Summary of the Law," quoting Deuteronomy 6:5 (love God with all your heart, soul, strength, and mind) and Leviticus 19:18 (love your neighbor as yourself). The Pharisee wanted to justify himself, so he asked Jesus, "And who is my neighbor?" Jesus then told the story we call the parable of the good Samaritan and ended with the charge "Go and do likewise."

I am sure that some positive thinker is now crying, "But didn't Jesus presuppose that I loved myself when he spoke?"

Remember that Jesus was quoting from a passage that begins, "Be holy because I, the LORD your God, am holy" (Leviticus 19:2) and follows this with a long list of laws that deal with sacrifice, ethical behavior, and justice and decency toward one another. The passage admonishes God's people

[2] Catherine Marshall, *Beyond Our Selves* (New York: Avon Books, 1974), p. 17.

not to pervert justice or show favoritism toward the great, but to judge neighbors fairly (19:15), to refrain from spreading slander or doing anything that endangers a neighbor's life (19:16), to refrain from hating one's brother in one's heart and to rebuke a neighbor frankly for sin (19:17), to eschew revenge or grudge-holding, and to love our neighbors as ourselves. (Read Leviticus 19:1-37 to understand this passage better.)

What is presupposed here is that one takes care of one's basic needs and takes reasonable care of oneself without fraud, harm, danger, or slandering one's own name. Self-love, in this sense, does not mean being fond of or even approving of ourselves; as C. S. Lewis says, ". . . Love for ourselves does not mean that we like ourselves. It means we wish our own good."[3] Don't we wish our own good even when we are disgusted with our own bad? Well, we can do that for others, too. In the Bible, it is called *agape*—charity—and it has nothing to do with approval or affection.

When I speak to Christian groups, I find that the hardest thing for them to accept is the idea that we are asked to love other people, whether or not we love ourselves. Since so many books have flooded the market about self-love, the church is in danger of absorbing this social theory into the gospel. I am ashamed to say that I hear self-pitying Christians insist, "Well, when I'm all healed from my hurts and can love myself, maybe I'll be able to help others."

But the message of Scripture is pretty clear: we should expect a lot from ourselves but be tender-hearted toward others, irrespective of how disgusted we are with our own shortcomings that day. In his epistle to the Romans, Paul says,

> We who are strong ought to bear with the failings of the weak, and not to please ourselves. Each of us should please his neighbor for his good, to build him up. For even Christ did not please himself . . . (Romans 15:1-3).

Myth: Self-love is a Christian virtue.

Jesus said—to a crowd of disciples, interested Jews who had heard about the raising of Lazarus, and Greeks who came to Jerusalem to Passover—

[3] C. S. Lewis, *Mere Christianity* (New York: Macmillan, Inc., 1960), p. 115.

"The man who loves his life will lose it, while the man who hates his life in this world will keep it for eternal life. Whoever serves me must follow me; and where I am, my servant will also be. My Father will honor the one who serves me" (John 12:25-26).

The great saints of God were rarely those who were preoccupied with self-love. In fact, usually any moment of adoration or recognition of God's greatness is followed immediately with some self-loathing. For instance, when Isaiah saw his vision of God, his immediate reaction was to cry, "Woe to me! . . . I am ruined! For I am a man of unclean lips, and I live among a people of unclean lips, and my eyes have seen the King, the LORD Almighty" (Isaiah 6:5). And when Peter was called to discipleship through the miracle of a great catch of fish, he cried, "Go away from me, Lord! I am a sinful man!" (Luke 5:8).

Many people who literally do hate their own lives can still love God. For instance, Paul said of himself, after a discourse on his own frailty in sin, "What a wretched man I am! Who will rescue me from this body of death? Thanks be to God—through Jesus Christ our Lord" (Romans 7:23-24). John Bunyan, who never liked himself much but who was captivated by the person of Jesus, wrote from prison, "I find to this day seven evils in my heart."[4] John Newton in his hymn "Amazing Grace" referred to himself as "a wretch." C. S. Lewis wrote, "In my most clear-sighted moments not only do I not think myself a nice man, but I know that I am a very nasty one."[5]

In fact, the more one studies the lives of great saints and martyrs and prophets, the more one finds a portrait of self-loathing—and a reminder that humility calls upon God's forgiving love.

Myth: We need to feel good about ourselves.

The Pharisees were men who felt good about themselves. They had clear consciences, constantly congratulated themselves on their righteousness, and even prayed in terms of their moral superiority, like the one who said, "God, I thank you that I am not like all other men—robbers, evildoers, adulterers—or even like this tax collector. I fast twice a week and give a tenth of all I get" (Luke 18:11-12). But it was the tax collector—a man who didn't even feel good enough about himself to look up toward heaven and whose prayer was one

[4] John Bunyan, *Grace Abounding* (Chicago: Moody Press, 1959), p. 119.
[5] Lewis, *Mere Christianity*, p. 105.

begging God to have mercy on him, a sinner—who went home "justified before God. For everyone who exalts himself will be humbled, and he who humbles himself will be exalted" (18:14).

"Feeling good about ourselves" can, in fact, be a verbal cover-up for self-indulgence; and this can become greed and avarice and, finally, the prideful state of full-fledged egotism. It was about this process that Jesus said,

> "Woe to you, teachers of the law and Pharisees, you hypocrites! You clean the outside of the cup and dish, but inside they are full of greed and self-indulgence. Blind Pharisee! First clean the inside of the cup and dish, and then the outside also will be clean" (Matthew 23:25-26).

I suspect that I am most dangerous to myself spiritually when I feel best about myself. I am most available to temptation when I ride the high horse of my own ego. Though I may rationalize that I'm only being "joyful in the Lord" when I'm high on praise and attention after a successful workshop or speaking date, these are the most spiritually dangerous times. While beaming at my admirers and autographing books, I might ignore someone pulling on the hem of my garment. Worse, I could begin substituting my pleasure in myself for the peace that passeth understanding, found only in Christ.

We all tend to enjoy the company of those who love us and admire us—because they make us feel good. But wasn't being self-satisfied the kind of sin Jesus hated? Rather, those who came to him feeling wretched and humble—like the Canaanite woman, who offered to eat the crumbs that fell to the dogs (Matthew 15:22-28)—seemed to gain his approval.

Christian love is perhaps summed up in the example of the woman who washed Jesus' feet with her tears, anointed them, and dried them with her hair (Luke 7:36-50). It is obvious that she wasn't pleased with the life she had led until then and that her only real joy was in the Master's forgiveness. Jesus said that she would be remembered, not for any happy feelings she had about herself or the life she led, but because "she loved much."

Christianity is not an analgesic that prevents us from feeling pain about ourselves. What it does do is give us peace in the middle of recognizing our own shortcomings, not because we feel good about ourselves, but because we feel good about Jesus and his work of salvation for us.

58 BEING A CHRISTIAN FRIEND

Myth: All God asks is that I love my neighbor as myself.

God would undoubtedly be pleased if we really *did* all love our neighbors as ourselves. The world would be more peaceful, and there would be no poor, lonely, distressed people among us. That would be wonderful!

But this message about loving our neighbors was given first in the Old Covenant; when Jesus quoted it, he was talking to Pharisees and teachers of the law. The love he asked Christians to have is usually called the New Commandment:

> "As the Father has loved me, so have I loved you. Now remain in my love.... My command is this: Love each other as I have loved you. Greater love has no one than this, that one lay down his life for his friends" (John 15:9-13).

What a different kind of love there is in this New Commandment! Christ loved us enough to take the blame for our sins, to accomplish the work of reconciliation, to become the very curse that would have fallen on us; he loved us enough to be whipped, mocked, spit on, crucified, and killed. Was this loving us (his neighbors) as himself—or was it loving us far more than he cared for his own life?

This is what Jesus says friends will do for one another: they will be willing, as they remain in his love, to suffer and die for one another. There is no possibility of deciding whether the friend would do it for us, in turn, or whether the friend is worth it anyhow. The apostle Thomas couldn't have said, "I'll die for Peter but not James," because Jesus said that love was his commandment.

Is this relevant today? Should we die for our friends? If we choose to be a friend of Jesus, then we must keep this new law, because he said in the next breath, "You are my friends if you do what I command" (John 15:14). We can't say, "I'll die for the Protestants but not for the Catholics," or, "... for the Baptists but not for the Lutherans," or, "... for the Democrats but not for the Republicans," or, "... for the people of America but not the people of El Salvador or South Africa." We can't say these things because Jesus is the perfect offering for our sins—and not for our sins only, but for the sins of the whole world (1 John 2:2).

I once heard an unchurched, intelligent man say that it looked to him as if a Christian was someone who loved Jesus and hated everyone else. Obviously, his experience with Christians wasn't a good one. While we, as Christians, investigate the epistle written by the Beloved Disciple, it is wise to consider these verses:

> Do not love the world or anything in the world. If anyone loves the world, the love of the Father is not in him (1 John 2:15).

> This is how we know what love is: Jesus Christ laid down his life for us. And we ought to lay down our lives for our brothers. If anyone has material possessions and sees his brother in need but has no pity on him, how can the love of God be in him? (3:16-17).

> We love because he first loved us. If anyone says, "I love God," yet hates his brother, he is a liar. For anyone who does not love his brother, whom he has seen, cannot love God, whom he has not seen. And he has given us this command: Whoever loves God must also love his brother (4:19-21).

Strange. In all these passages about loving God and loving one another, John didn't say a thing about loving ourselves. Perhaps he just didn't understand modern psychology, or perhaps he knew something the world can't understand.

7

How to Tell a Friend from an Alligator

When Job's three friends, Eliphaz of Teman, Bildad of Shuah, and Zophar of Naamah, heard all these calamities which had overtaken him, they left their homes and arranged to come and condole with him and comfort him (Job 2:11, NEB).

My grandson Andrew was riding in my car one day when he was almost three. Strapped into his safety seat directly behind me as I drove, he called out his comments on the cherry trees, passing motorcycles, blackbirds, light poles, and other fascinating sights and noises. Then he was silent for a while, thinking; finally, he said, "Gra'mother?"

"Yes, Andrew?"

"Gra'mother, a dog is a friend!"

"Yes," I said. "A dog is a friend."

There was another period of silence, and then he called out, "Gra'mother?"

"Yes, Andrew?"

"A cat is a friend!" he said.

"Yes, Andrew," I agreed. "A cat is a friend."

There was a much longer silence, and then as I turned the

corner into our cul-de-sac, he cried out, "Gra'mother!"

"Yes, Andrew?"

"Gra'mother, I don't think an alligator is a friend," he said with sad certainty.

An alligator is not a friend! You might half-tame one of these crafty reptiles and keep it as a sort of pet. But even if it swam in your bathtub, you'd never completely trust it, because alligators are not affectionate, interdependent with humans, or domesticated. They don't have the disposition that thousands of years of cooperation with people have created in dogs, cats, cows, and horses.

Each of us has probably had an experience with an Alligator in our relationships. Job's three celebrated "comforters" were Alligators. Judas became an Alligator. Saul was a dangerous Alligator, until he met Jesus on the Damascus road.

Alligators like these turn up in everyday life, not just in the Bible. There are some things friends just don't do to one another—but there are people who shock and surprise us by doing them. Our inevitable reaction, if we have any opportunity for recourse, is to turn to that person and say, "But I thought we were friends!"

Does this mean that you should be on guard, examining every candidate for friendship?

No, especially if you don't need new friends or if you are now deliberately being a fool for Christ, living intentionally, giving all you have, knowing that you expect nothing in return, and becoming the kind of person Paul called himself in 1 Corinthians 4:10.

Yes, to an extent, if you are in need of particular companionship, if you are friend-seeking, looking for a bird of your own feather to flock with, not so much to minister as simply to be a more fulfilled part of God's kingdom. If this is where you are, you need to be on guard against being bitten by some kinds of Alligators.

Usually, one or two incidents of betrayal or disappointment make us a little more discriminating about entering the unknown of friendship too quickly. Discrimination is wisdom, not paranoia, and it should spring more from spiritual discernment than from worldly knowledge. We should strive to be as innocent as doves and as wise as snakes, according to Jesus (Matthew 10:16). He was warning his disciples of the power of other people to be set against them in their ministry; in other words, he told them to watch out for Alligators.

On the other hand, we must be quick to forgive Alligators for the bites that we do sustain. If we don't forgive people who hurt us, we bind their wickedness for judgment and place ourselves in danger as well (see John 20:23; Matthew 16:19). When Jesus presented the Lord's Prayer in the Sermon on the Mount, he followed it with the admonition "For if you forgive men when they sin against you, your heavenly Father will also forgive you. But if you do not forgive men their sins, your Father will not forgive your sins" (Matthew 6:14-15).

This doesn't mean that we have to keep letting people hurt us. I would be foolish to go wading barefoot in the Everglades where alligators are lurking; I would be even more foolish to say to each one who bit me, "I forgive you, so bite me again." To do so would not make me a fool for Christ—it would show me to be a masochist. We can always forgive, but we don't have to continue to associate with Alligators, no matter how much we love them.

Amazingly, there are some people who never seem to learn how to tell the difference between friends and Alligators. These folks constantly find themselves betrayed, let down, gossiped about, stolen from, cheated, and blamed for things they didn't do, all by people who, for example, couldn't stand closeness, so they either struck out at the friend, were unable to maintain their end of a friendship, or were clever manipulators who used friendship for their own ends.

Intolerance for Closeness

Those who can't stand closeness often send double messages. They say, "Let's be best friends!" while reacting to any open sharing or intimate friendship with strong negativity. Most of these people would like to be friends; they are Alligators in spite of themselves. They've been emotionally crippled in childhood and aren't able to enter deep relationships.

"But shouldn't I try to be her friend for those very reasons," asks a loving Christian woman, "so that I can help to undo the damage of her childhood?"

The answer is that you should be a friend *to* such persons as long as you don't expect to be friends *with* them. "Do not resist an evil person," Jesus told people who listened on the Mount of Olives (Matthew 5:39). He did not mean you to risk your salvation in Christ for another but to be open, loving, and giving, expecting nothing in return.

Most of us don't do this with a very good will, at least not for long. Don't turn the other cheek to someone if you're going to resent it afterwards. You *must* act in total love, in total obedience to Christ, when you sacrifice yourself for friendship. If it's done to make yourself look or feel good or to make the friend love you more, it's neurotic and unscriptural. Be authentically what you are and where you are in your Christian walk; don't try to be a martyr if martyrdom makes you angry.

Furthermore, be careful that you don't make someone worse, instead of better, with your love. I wouldn't give an alcoholic a bottle of whiskey, no matter how much I loved her or him. If I had an Alligator friend who, say, criticized me unmercifully about everything I did and said, I wouldn't indulge her just because her mother was mean to her when she was a child; nor would I stand still and let someone abuse me physically, excusing his violence because his father was a tyrant. That wouldn't help me or the friend.

Unless you have extensive counseling skills or are a health professional, you may be playing with fire if you try digging into your friend's past for details to "free them for friendship." If prayer and submission to the Lord lead you to such a person, prepare to be a careful, gentle friend without trying for too much depth, or expecting reciprocal love. These Alligators seem unconsciously to draw as much life and love as possible from friendship and then suddenly "garbage-dump" on their friends. Some even complain to others that our gestures of friendship are improper or embarrassing!

My young friend Ruthie entered what looked like a delightful friendship with Candace, a Christian neighbor. They seemed to have everything in common, including weaving and playing the flute. Their children were close in age, and Ruthie and Candace even attended the same church. But suddenly, after a few months of making rugs together, playing flute duets, and studying the Bible, the Alligator spirit emerged in Candace.

Her father was a hard, strict fundamentalist pastor, and her mother was much like him; so Candace had been treated with coldness and punished harshly as a child. Unable, because of her upbringing, to cope with any imperfection in herself or her children, she suddenly saw terrible flaws in Ruthie. She turned on Ruthie, discussing her shortcomings with their mutual friends at church and even suggesting that Ruthie was making improper or homosexual overtures with her frequent hugs!

This Alligator was a sort of Pharisee; she had been so roughly treated for all her own transgressions and so well-trained to see sin (whether it existed or not) that she imagined it in others. Furthermore, she not only judged Ruthie but executed Ruthie's punishment by defaming her name and rejecting her.

Frailty in Maintaining Relationships

Then there is a kind of Alligator who simply doesn't have the spiritual and psychological grounding in character to maintain a friendship. These are like seeds sown in rocky soil—they spring up quickly but are scorched in the hot sun and die because their roots are shallow (Matthew 13:5-6). These unhardy types leap quickly into closeness, but when the hot sun of deepening friendship shines, they wither up and seem unable to do their part.

People who try to be friends with these emotionally and spiritually fragile people find themselves making all the effort, all the gestures of love, all the calls and trips and arrangements. Why? Not because rocky-soil Alligators are wicked, but because they just don't have the energy to follow through and they get scared easily.

I knew a young man once who was such a person. Because Larry was in a church youth group for which I was advisor, over several years I saw him initiate or respond eagerly to friendships with both girls and other boys in the church, going to dinner at their homes and acting as if God had blessed him greatly "at last" with real friends.

But each time, usually within a few weeks, the other person in the relationship would tell me, "I don't understand it. I thought we were friends, but he suddenly seemed to lose interest and drift off." If it was one of the girls in the group, they would come for counsel, saying anxiously, "What did I do wrong? We had two dates, and I thought we were getting along beautifully, but he never called me again."

These people are so spiritually slender and so emotionally shallow that—although they love the company, the gift-giving, the greeting cards, and the sympathetic counsel of friends—they can't take real depth or return the favors for long. Rocky-soil seedlings wither in heat, remember? And rocky-soil Alligators can't stand the heat of their own feelings; so if they find themselves becoming dependent on or falling in love with a member of the opposite sex, they shrink away. So if you're sick or your teenagers are driving you crazy or your business is in trouble and you need someone to comfort you, look somewhere else.

Again, if you want to be a friend to this person, God will bless you. Rocky-soil people don't usually change much, but with God, all things are possible. You will be acting like Christ if you continue to be friendly to this kind of person; just don't expect to find the joys of mutual love in the relationship. You'll be the full-time giver.

Some Alligators, however, were victims themselves. These are people who have never forgotten being hurt by friends or parents or spouses. Somebody somewhere betrayed them or let them down or used them, and now they're afraid to enter other deep relationships. They refuse to make long-term commitments—often to marriage or parenthood or even a job—because they continue to respond to a signal from the past.

This is a sign of immaturity and inability to carry out a friendship; carried to extreme, it is the sin of grudge-holding and can become a grave mental or character disorder. I know a man whose best friend borrowed money from him, took advantage of his hospitality, and then stole the car he had loaned him and ran off with his wife! The victim in this story was rightfully wary of others for a time; but if he had continued this way, judging all offerings of friendship by his past trauma, he would have been emotionally and spiritually stagnant, living by past experience alone.

Justification for Antisocial Behavior

The bite of an Alligator can sometimes infect others (just as, in the movies of the thirties, a person bitten by a vampire became a vampire, too!). This kind of unhappy person, originally an Alligator's victim, reacts differently from most hurt people.

Instead of becoming fearful, this type might develop into the worst kind of Alligator. Because of real or imagined injustices either in childhood or in later-life experience, this individual seems to feel all right about stealing or lying or cheating. He or she has passed sentence on the human race and feels justified in engaging in what we call antisocial behavior. Fortunately, there aren't a lot of these people around, but they can play havoc with good lives.

Do such people turn up in churches? Unfortunately, they occasionally do. "Con artists," manipulators, and cheats sometimes use the church as a place to operate. Others, who are not as steeped in evil, may be honestly trying to change through the ministry of the church, but they may have a relapse of this terrible Alligator fever.

Confusing Game Playing

Then there are the game players, who probably mean well but leave a wake of confusion behind them. Some years ago one of my daughters had an acquaintance whose Alligator way showed itself in a strange friendship game that I call "Help me, help me, help me; stop forcing your help on me." Most of us do it occasionally to some extent, but in its extreme form, this activity can ruin a friendship.

Cindy was a pleasant, quick young woman with a stolid, silent husband. They attended a church that put great emphasis on the man's participation in church affairs, and so the elders and older women of the congregation were trying to change her so that her husband could "come out of his shell." Cindy's house was papered with Bible verses about submission and the silence of women. According to her church's theory, if she became weaker and more dependent and unspeaking, her husband would suddenly emerge from his stolidness, start helping to run the church, and speak at the prophet level.

Periodically, Cindy would become disenchanted and tell my daughter how she longed to use her own considerable skills in her church and home. She even suggested that her marriage was shaky because resentment built up between her and her husband over this need to change each other. After these sessions my daughter might suggest that Cindy concentrate on pleasing God, not people, and pray for guidance rather than taking so much advice. The girl would then rush to her husband and church friends and tell them that they and my daughter were confusing her with such contrary counsel. There would always be an uproar. Finally, after one of these little circles of reaction, Cindy called my daughter and said, "My husband has forbidden me to be friends with you any longer because you're trying to confuse what the Lord is telling me, and I know he's right."

Jealous Possession and Remaking

Perhaps the worst kind of Alligators are the jealous, possessive friends who want us all to themselves. If they are new to our lives, these possessive friends seem to resent our lifetime friends, quickly pointing out their faults and even sometimes saying insulting things to them when we're all together. If this is an Alligator we've known for years, he or she can sometimes seem to scuttle any new friends that come along. A jealous friend is really not a true friend; true friends would put our happiness as a higher priority than exclusiveness in a relationship.

Though they live in different cities, Maggie and Lise had been friends for several years. They had been roommates at a Christian college and bridesmaids in each other's weddings. They and their husbands barbecued, played bridge, and went to church together until Lise and her husband Jack were transferred to another city.

Everything was fine at first, even though they were separated; the two friends wrote often, and Maggie and Ted went to visit Lise and Jack and had a wonderful time. But eventually, Lise made new friends, and Maggie was heartbroken. Ted brought her home from their last visit in tears. She was depressed for weeks because she could see her friendship with Lise changing from "best friend" status to a kind of "back burner" sentiment and loyalty that most old friends in separate parts of the country feel for one another.

Maggie wrote several confusing letters to Lise and called her on the telephone, crying out in many ways, "Please don't forget me." But instead of heating up the friendship, Maggie's neurotic and unchristian behavior cooled Lise's feelings. Finally, they had a showdown on the telephone one night, and Lise said, "Maggie, even God doesn't try to dominate my life the way you want to. At least God gave me free will!"

Maggie hasn't heard from Lise since that night, now about a year ago. And because she doesn't look carefully in the mirror of truth that God gives us all, she still doesn't see that she has grown Alligator scales.

Some friends are possessive in different ways. Phil wasn't jealous in his friendship with Gordon; he just wanted Gordon to become someone else. He was always trying to change his friend and used God as a voice for his ideals.

"I know the Lord wants you to quit being so careless with money," he would say and then follow this comment with an appropriate Scripture. He went on to try to remake Gordon's life into what he believed was a Christian ideal, criticizing Gordon's eating habits, his job performance, and even his marriage. Phil was heartbroken when Gordon ended the friendship.

"We've had fights about this before, but I always knew that Gordon would see that I was right in the end," he moaned. "Shouldn't friends correct one another, especially when the Lord guides them?" With that, he pulled out a few "correction" Scriptures. Phil wasn't a bad person, just a blind one, and Jesus was rather firm about what happens when the blind try to be guides (see Matthew 23:16).

Remember that friends love and accept one another. If they see us committing what seems to be a grave wrong, they may confront us, but they don't try to rearrange our personalities, like Phil, or try to turn others against us, like Candace.

Alligators are never satisfied with one bite; after correcting a friend harshly, they usually run straight to other mutual friends or acquaintances. Or they rush to the friend's clergy for "counseling," through which they can discredit the friend's own ministry.

The Difference Between Friends and Alligators

Friends offer solutions; they don't just find fault. This is something we all need to remember so that we don't start growing thick hides and pointed teeth. I am reminded of this when I visit a friend who is the sloppiest person I've ever known. When I visit, I have to scrape a month's accumulation of magazines, stained coffee cups, pencils, newspapers, bread crusts, and usually a cat or two, off a chair, just so I can sit down. Here is where my love for her is put on its mettle, because as a daughter of God I have only two choices. I can either accept and love her as she is, drinking tea from a cup that looks like a laboratory culture and ignoring her personal untidiness as none of my business, or I can confess my discomfort and offer to help her clean up, acknowledging that she is physically not very strong, that she herself might wish she wasn't in such a mess, and that she could probably use some help.

Any other behavior on my part would be pure alligatorishness. Alligators often use someone's flaws as a basis for enmity and hold up perfection as a basis for friendship, saying, "If only you'd. . . ." instead of either, "Stay the way you are" or "Can I help?"

One of the quickest ways to tell a friend from an Alligator is to ask yourself the following questions. If any of your answers is yes, you may be dealing with an amphibious reptile!

1. Do I have to make major changes in myself to gain or keep this person as a friend?

2. Does my friend often act jealous or sulky or moody when we're with others?

3. Does he or she take advantage of our friendship or behave inconsiderately, borrowing money I can't really afford to lend, calling at late hours, or dropping by too often when I'm busy? Does my friend seem to resent it when I can't drop everything for him or her?

4. Does it seem as if my friend wants to come between me and my spouse, my parents, or my children?

5. Do I wish that he or she would return some of my favors?

6. Do I seem to make all the effort in our friendship?

7. Does my friend seem to elicit all my secrets, while keeping his or her own life more guarded?

8. Am I ever uncomfortable or on my guard with this person?

9. Does my friend seem to know what God wants for me better than I do?

10. Have I ever heard a secret that I had told my friend come out of someone else's mouth so that I knew my confidence had been betrayed?

Recently, Micki, an acquaintance of mine, was completely devastated by an Alligator bite. Her best "friend" had suddenly turned on her, betrayed her to others, and ended their relationship. I spent a couple of hours one morning comforting and counseling Micki. That afternoon, while I was in a bookstore, I thought of looking for something that might help her through the hard time.

I found an interesting book on surviving a loss. It dealt with loss of spouse by death or divorce, loss of a lover, loss of a job or a home, loss of hair or teeth, or money in the stock market, and so on. The only loss that wasn't named was the loss of a friend.

"Why?" I asked myself all the way home. "Why didn't it deal with a friend like Micki's?"

The answer came suddenly. The book didn't need to deal with the loss of a friend through betrayal because friends don't treat each other that way. Micki wasn't grieving for a friend. She was crying over an Alligator.

8

Some Friendships in the Old Testament

> *We have heard with our ears, O God;*
> *our fathers have told us*
> *what you did in their days,*
> *in days long ago.*
> —*Psalm 44:1*

There are as many kinds of friendship in the Bible as there are in modern life. The relationships described in the Bible were, like our own friendships, often paradoxical. David wrote a number of psalms about disloyalty and wickedness of enemies, but his tragic relationship with Jonathan is often used as a magnificent example of brotherly affection. Deborah tongue-lashed Barak for cowardice; yet she accompanied him into battle, just as a friend might (Judges 4).

The Old Testament is especially rich in tales of the interaction of friends. Esther and her older cousin Mordecai were friends, united in their fervor to save the Jewish people (Esther 2:5-17; 3); Esther's husband, on the other hand, was manipulated by his oily-tongued companions. Deuteronomy 14:6 warns people against being enticed by a close friend to worship other gods; so this must have been a fairly common problem. Samson lost his Philistine wife to a friend (the KJV says, "whom he had used as his friend") after his friends had "plowed with his heifer" (Judges 14:18-20). Micah made friends with a Levite—in fact, he installed him as priest and father—but the Levite wanted a big congregation more than he wanted Micah's gentle friendship (Judges 17:7–18:26). Ezra and Nehemiah made friends with the rulers of Persia and rebuilt the walls of Jerusalem.

Some of these are just interesting stories about real people, but others have a second meaning; they shed light on our own relationships with one another. As we examine a few of the companions in Scripture, perhaps we can gain insight into our own lives.

Adam and Eve (Genesis 1–3; 4:25-26)

When the world and everything in it were created, God brought the divine spirit of love and friendship into that creation. Viewing the man, God said, "I think he's lonely, and that's not good. I'll make him a friend, a partner."

We often dwell on the negatives about Adam and Eve, unable to see anything but their disobedience and expulsion from the garden. Adam and Eve behaved very much like two children who are friends. First, they got into more mischief together than they ever did singly. Then, Adam tried to put the blame on Eve. They tried to hide together from God because they were exposed (in more ways than one!), and they sewed some fig leaves together to cover their mutual embarrassments. This story sounds almost like some of the plots my own children hatched when they could garner a little support from their friends!

But not only were Adam and Eve the first sinners; they were the first people to live by God's breath, which made them a part of God, even if they were no longer able to eat from the Tree of Life. And then they became the first farmers and first parents. Since these first two people were created to speak directly with God, it was during their lifetimes and the lifetimes of their son Seth and their grandson Enosh that people began "first to invoke the name of Yahweh" (see Genesis 4:24-26, *The Jerusalem Bible*). Besides being the first people and farmers and parents and sinners, Adam and Eve were the first friends.

Whether you think the Eden story is the absolute, literal

truth or a poetic hymn about God's relationship to humanity, it is still an all-important story because Adam and Eve are shown living out all the relationships that we now call friends, partners, lovers, spouses, co-workers—and the Church (worshipers of God in a congregation of two). Whom else did they have?

Eden is a significant situation for us in the present time, because "the LORD God said, 'It is not good for the man to be alone. I will provide a partner for him' " (Genesis 2:18, NEB).

In this act of creative decision God gave us the imperative to companionship. It isn't good for people to be alone all the time; and there are times—especially when we fall from grace or make terrible decisions or lose everything—that we need someone else, like a friend or a spouse, to help us bear our burdens.

I'm aware that God has apparently called some people to be hermits or monks or nuns or to go into lonely professions; but even they usually have occasional conclaves with others like themselves. We all need to be alone part of the time; but nobody needs to be alone forever. Perhaps that's why in prisons solitary confinement is considered to be such a hard punishment.

The Builders at Babel (Genesis 11:1-11)

I once heard a remarkable sermon in which a renowned ecumenist laughed, "The Tower of Babel is an example of what we could do if only we would join together with one will."

The fellows at Babel were most assuredly friends, at least until they all began to speak gibberish to one another (which probably frustrated them to the point of fistfights). They had one common goal: to make a name for themselves, apparently with no help from God.

Their sin was not, as we are inclined to believe, their trying to get to heaven by building a tall building. God might have laughed at their folly, but there is no place in Scripture where people were punished for wanting to get to heaven or for seeking the elusive face of God, even if they did so foolishly. If anything, God would probably have permitted some kind of theophany to take place or sent an angel to give them a hand.

No, it wasn't their building toward heaven that angered God. It was their craving for fame, for a memorial to their own greatness so that they wouldn't be lost from one another. These people were smitten by pride, and they built a monument to it. (Maybe you'd like to read the passage again; see especially verse 4.)

At any rate, Babel symbolizes what happens when ambition and friendship bake bricks and stir tar: confusion sets in and God is glorified only when the friendship ends. The danger was clear: "The Lord said, 'If as one people speaking the same language they have begun to do this, then nothing they plan to do will be impossible for them'" (Genesis 11:6).

This is the kind of arrogant relationship that caused the downfall of a few religious leaders who threw in their lots with ambitious kings and still occasionally causes some holy people, like evangelists and gospel singers and preachers, to go astray together. Sometimes God has to intervene again. At Babel, and sometimes in modern friendships, God says, "This is unhealthy and unholy, and I won't have it!"

Abraham, the Friend for All Seasons (Genesis 12–25)

How sweet the friendship between Abraham and God looks to us now! But in those days, we might have thought Abraham to be a bit eccentric if not downright ridiculous.

Because of his friendship with God, whom nobody could see, Abram dragged his wife, servants, some relatives, and large herds of sheep and cattle from somewhere in Akkad to Haran to Canaan to Egypt and back to Canaan. Even worse, he suddenly changed his name to Abraham and was seen talking to the air. He mutilated himself with a stone knife, twice claimed that his wife was his sister, and even tried to sacrifice his own son!

But Abraham is counted as God's friend because he loved the One who spoke convincingly out of the whirlwind and he went where God directed him to go. Abraham, who covenanted with God as two friends might draw up a contract, was also a good friend to others.

He perhaps risked his own skin by pleading with God for Sodom, carrying the plea on and on, for Lot's sake. He treated Sarah as an adult with privilege, rather than as chattel, when he said, "Hagar is your slave. Do what you think is best." He was fair in the land division with Lot and asked God for a redress of grievance over Ishmael. He sent some costly bride-gifts with his son's matchmaker so that Isaac would be seen with honor in his father's land. He gave his concubines and his second wife's sons handsome gifts while he was still alive, and he did not take advantage of his friendship with the Hittites over the price of Sarah's burial cave in Machpelah.

Two of the rather sparse Old Testament uses of the word "friend" are about Abraham: "O our God, did you not . . . give [the land] forever to the descendants of Abraham your friend?" (2 Chronicles 20:7) and "But you, O Israel, my servant, Jacob, whom I have chosen, you descendants of Abraham my friend . . ." (Isaiah 41:8).

Abraham through his friendship with God became better than he was; he left us a legacy, a clue that we, too, can somehow become friends with the Creator of the universe, letting that friendship be the touchstone for being friends with others.

Jacob and Laban (Genesis 29–31)

One might wonder if the story of Jacob and Laban was included in the Torah as an example of how not to conduct a relationship.

Both were wily thieves and tricksters. (Maybe they were both part Alligator!) Jacob was hiding out in Paddan Aram in the first place because of his brother Esau's wrath over two tricks Jacob had pulled: getting Esau's right of primogeniture with a bowl of lentil stew and plotting with their mother to secure the blessing on the firstborn from their father. So when we feel sorry for Jacob in his relationship with Laban, we should remember not to grieve too deeply. Jacob, the father of the Twelve Tribes, was also inclined to be a mama's boy, and God loved him for reasons we might argue with, except for the few glimpses of his better side: the dream of the ladder, the seven years' work that "seemed like only a few days" to Jacob because he was so in love, or his exquisite grief over Joseph. There are as many theories as there are theologians, and we aren't really sure just why Jacob was the chosen twin.

Laban, meanwhile, had two problems. First, his older daughter Leah was getting past the age of nubility and didn't appeal to Jacob. So Laban gave him a dose of his own trickery by substituting Leah for Rachel on the wedding night just as cleverly as Jacob had wrapped his arms in goatskin and substituted himself for Esau to obtain Isaac's blessing.

Second, there was a labor problem in Paddan Aram, and

Laban apparently couldn't hire a good overseer cheaply enough; so he found a way to get Jacob to work fourteen years for him with no more pay than having his two daughters for wives.

I suspect that in their conniving way Jacob and Laban rather liked and respected each other, at least until the matter of property came up. By the time he asked to be released from his bond, Jacob had two wives, two concubines, and thirteen children that we know of, and there was always some kind of trouble going on between the wives. Laban responded to the request for release in one of those particularly fascinating barter exchanges in Scripture (Abraham buying Machpelah is another):

"Please, don't leave," Laban said unctuously. "I have found out by divination that because of your presence, God has blessed me. So, decide how much you want for your work."

This all sounded very fair, except that Jacob *knew* Laban (and vice versa).

"I don't want a dime," said Jacob. "I was glad to do it for you and your family, but I want to do something for my own family now."

"Anything," said Laban. "Name it."

"No, I don't want gifts, even though I've knocked myself out for you all these years. But how about letting me have all the culls and miscolored animals?"

Laban apparently thought that if Jacob wanted a bunch of runt sheep and goats with discolored wool that sold for less, it was okay. In fact, he may have expected Jacob to have second thoughts, because he then traveled three days' distance from his son-in-law. But he obviously didn't count on Jacob using some kind of Canaanite folk magic to make the ewes and doe goats drop all those big, healthy, spotted lambs and kids and then make separate flocks, with all the one-color, weak, spindly animals going to Laban.

Laban's sons (who suddenly reappear in Genesis 31 after an absence of several chapters) began to bad-mouth Jacob and point out to their father that Jacob was getting rich on the fat of their land. And Jacob noticed, after that report, that "Laban's attitude toward him was not what it had been" (31:2). Their friendship began to take on a new complexion.

You probably know the rest of the story. God intervened for

Jacob one more time and told him to get back to Canaan immediately. So Jacob loaded up some camels and took off with children, wives, flocks, and some household gods that he didn't know were hidden in the luggage. Laban, already warned by God to be careful, pursued them. When he caught up with Jacob's caravan, he recited his grievance:

> "What have you done? You've deceived me, and you've carried off my daughters like captives in war. Why did you run off secretly and deceive me? Why didn't you tell me, so I could send you away with joy and singing to the music of tambourines and harps? You didn't even let me kiss my grandchildren and my daughters good-by. You have done a foolish thing. I have the power to harm you; but last night the God of your father said to me, 'Be careful not to say anything to Jacob, either good or bad.' Now you have gone off because you long to return to your father's house. But why did you steal my gods?" (31:26-30).

(I never felt particularly sorry for Laban until I became a grandmother; then the line "you didn't even let me kiss my grandchildren" struck me like a stone!)

The two men had a long, strained conversation after this accusation. They were probably saved from ending in blows when Laban made his wonderfully Middle-Eastern suggestion: "Let's make a covenant."

The heaping of the stones at Mizpah was to serve as a watchtower between two friends who have agreed to disagree. "This is a sign of a covenant," the stones said. "And God is watching to make sure we keep it." The agreement was that Jacob wouldn't take any other wives or mistreat Laban's daughters and Laban wouldn't go past the stones to make war on Jacob's tribes.

The Mizpah prayer said, "May God be the judge as to how well we keep the covenant." (I'm amused to note that church groups use the Mizpah "blessing" to show their love for one another and lovers sometimes buy halves of a coin inscribed with the words. The Mizpah covenant was not made in love; it was made in the fear of God and in respect for Isaac and for Jacob's wives.) A tower of stones is an arms limitation treaty between former friends who were not very good to each other in the first place.

The friendship that is based on mutual (or alternate) manipulation will never be an easy one. If you have such a relationship, maybe you'd better start collecting stones for Mizpah.

Elijah and Elisha (1 Kings 19:8-21; 2 Kings 1:1–2:18)

It's good to start with Elijah in the cave (after he had fled from Jezebel) before exploring his partnership with Elisha, because he had come to the end of one thing and the beginning of another while he was atop Mount Carmel. Elijah the Tishbite went to Horeb ostensibly to hide from the queen, but he was also tired, depressed, and dissolute. The prophet business certainly wasn't all roses; so maybe he even went there to hide from the Lord. It didn't work. The Lord's Word suddenly asked, "What are you doing here, Elijah?"

"I've been good!" Elijah cried, recounting his own zeal and the Israelites' apostasy. "I'm the only one left serving you, and now they're after me."

"Go confront God," said God. And Elijah confronted wind and fire and earthquake. Finally, he heard a gentle whisper—what the KJV calls the "still small voice"—and pulled his cloak over his head because he knew Who was speaking.

A few minutes later, he was told to go anoint a king for Syria and a new prophet for Israel. In other words, "Leave the punishment to my servants, Elijah, and don't think you're alone. I'll give you a partner, a trainee; I'll save seven thousand faithful; and then, when you've shown my strength to the king's army, I'll give you rest."

The vision of God's presence is always an imperative. God always says, "Look at me," before saying, "Go for me." Abraham heard God speak to him, Moses had the burning bush, and Isaiah saw heaven open, before they went where God sent them.

Elijah left the mountain with new strength and went straight to Elisha, who was plowing a field. Elijah threw his cloak over this son of Shaphat, and Elisha knew that a friendship ordained by God was at hand.

"Let me say good-bye to my family," he pled.

Elijah, who, I imagine, was always crusty, said, "What did I do? Did I tell you to come with me? Go home."

Elisha apparently took this as a pithy invitation of God's old prophet, and so he ran back and killed two (or twelve) oxen and barbecued them over a fire made out of his farming equipment, serving the meat as a farewell dinner. (First Kings makes this sound like a snack, but when you think about the time required to butcher those oxen, skin off the hides, prepare the meat for cooking, and roast it on a wood fire, the event must have lasted several days.) And then Elisha ran after Elijah.

Elisha, Elijah's friend and protegé, isn't mentioned again until 2 Kings 2. But as the prophet called down fire from heaven to consume Ahaziah's captains and then pronounced judgment on the king, we can imagine Elisha nearby; after all, this was Elijah's last act on earth for Yahweh. Sure enough, the second chapter shows them together, setting out for Gilgal. Elijah, hearing the approach of chariots with his inner ear, said he'd go to Bethel instead, and Elisha, like a true friend in God, said, "As surely as the LORD lives and as you live, I will not leave you" (2 Kings 2:2).

They went from Bethel to Jericho to the Jordan, repeating this conversation. Elijah miraculously parted the water by striking it with his cloak. He also showed his friendship for Elisha by managing to gather up some prophets to see the end, thus accrediting Elisha and eliminating the need for his protegé to proclaim himself as Elijah's heir.

"What can I leave you?" the old prophet asked in his gruff, loving way.

"A double portion of your spirit!" cried Elisha, who couldn't think of anything more wonderful. This is one of the sweetest passages between friends in all Scripture, and it contains the highest compliment one can pay.

"You *would* ask for the hardest thing possible," Elijah said. "If you watch me go and can see what happens, then you will have it."

> As they were walking along and talking together, suddenly a chariot of fire and horses of fire appeared and separated the two of them, and Elijah went up to heaven in a whirlwind. Elisha saw this, and cried out, "My father! My father! The chariots and horsemen of Israel!" (2:11-12).

"My father" is the Middle Eastern title of ultimate friendship and reverence, still used in those countries. Elisha cried out in a mixture of joy at Elijah's victory in God, sorrow for the loss of his friend, and hope for his own new ministry. He knew that because he saw God's army of Israel, perhaps led by

Michael himself, he was not only the new prophet but one who had received a "double portion."

Elisha even called his description of his vision up to the whirlwind to tell the disappearing Elijah, "Don't worry! I see the sign, so I have my wish." This was his blessing, to send Elijah to heaven in one of the most glorious moments in the Old Testament; then he perfunctorily rent his garments, to show proper respect. After that, he picked up the mantle that had fallen from Elijah's shoulders.

"Where is the LORD, the God of Elijah?" he cried, and he rapped the water of the Jordan with his new mantle so that he could go across and start his new life as prophet of Israel. The fifty prophets who were watching said, "The spirit of Elijah is resting on Elisha."

Moral: if you make friends with a prophet, you may be expected to carry on your friend's work.

A Common Thread in Old Testament Friendships

When we first read about the relationships of men and women in the Old Testament, we may find it difficult to discern any factor that is common to all of them. But with a little study we will probably notice that they are parts of a whole and that the whole is God's action in human history.

Adam and Eve set the scene for their own Fall (and therefore the fallen nature of humanity), the Law, and the Atonement. Their children, the men and women of Scripture, symbolize human ambition, the confusion we cause by our polemics, love and obedience that are examples of friendship with God, wiliness and plotting that are dangerous to friendship, and relationships that seem nearly perfect in God's sight.

In every one of the friendships recorded in Scripture, we see God reaching through these relationships to speak to sinful humans of the plan for history.

9

Friends of the New Covenant

> *Now about brotherly love we do not need to write to you, for you yourselves have been taught by God to love each other (1 Thessalonians 4:9).*

The history and letters of the New Covenant (New Testament) may sometimes seem idealized, perhaps because they were written down by people who, like Cleopas and his companion after their encounter with Christ on the road to Emmaus, asked themselves, "Didn't our hearts burn as he talked?" But the human friendship among those who followed Jesus—humanity transformed by association with God's Son—is impossible to hide even behind well-earned haloes.

Mary and Elizabeth (Luke 1:26-56)

Except for Jesus himself, there may be no greater example of unconditional response to God than that of Mary his mother, even though at first she was "greatly troubled" at Gabriel's deeply reverent, almost adoring greeting (Luke 1:28). But she questioned only the obvious, practical problem: "How can this be, when I'm still a virgin?" (see 1:34).

If angels tremble, Gabriel must have done so as he told

her, "The Holy Spirit will come upon you, and will overshadow you. . . ."

Mary could have refused, saying she didn't feel strong enough to face Joseph or her friends with this; she could have run from the angel, blaming the vision on her imagination; or she could even have ignored Gabriel when he came. But she said, "Yes!" without equivocation, and made herself not only servant but friend to God, and this friendship was one day to pierce her soul (Luke 2:35).

The friendship of Mary and her older kinswoman Elizabeth was marked by the quality found only in true Christian friendships: the relationship works to the glory of God. When Mary visited Elizabeth, she didn't just say, "Mary! How nice of you to come!" Instead, she cried, "But why am I favored, that the mother of my Lord should come to me?" And Mary responded by singing her great hymn, the Magnificat, in which God is extolled: "My soul doth magnify the Lord, and my spirit hath rejoiced in God my Saviour" (Luke 1:46-47, KJV).

Mary, like Abraham, was God's friend through her response to God's call. When she shared her miracle, her older cousin exclaimed, "Blessed is she who has believed that what the Lord has said to her will be accomplished!" One can have no greater friendship with Christ than to believe that his Word is true and to say, "Yes!" to him.

Joseph, Friend of Mary and Jesus

There are husbands and fathers who are so busy demanding their "rightful places" in the family that they forget to be friends with their wives and children. These men could take inspiration from Joseph the carpenter, who embodied spousal and parental friendship.

Few men would be able to accept the fact of a fiancée's pregnancy—particularly a pregnancy explained by a story of such unbelievable proportions. Yet when an angel appeared to Joseph in a dream, explaining that Mary had conceived by the Holy Spirit, he didn't ignore the dream as fantasy; instead, he listened and obeyed and took Mary as his wife (Matthew 1:19-24), thus sheltering her from the allotted punishment of being stoned to death for adultery. (Since Mary had already "given her troth" to Joseph, her status was that of a married woman; therefore, she would have been found guilty of adultery not just fornication.)

Joseph reverenced his wife by having no sexual union with her while she was pregnant. Instead of demanding his rights, this husband gave his wife and her unborn Son complete and unconditional love and acceptance. In fact, it was Joseph who gave the Baby the name Jesus (Matthew 1:25). Later he took Jesus to be presented in the temple at Jerusalem, where Joseph redeemed Jesus with "a pair of doves or two young pigeons," doing everything prescribed by the Law.

Joseph took Mary and Jesus to Egypt to escape Herod's wrath. When Joseph returned to Israel, he quietly settled in Nazareth so that the Judean ruler Archelaus would not notice the family (Matthew 2:21-23), even though he could probably have been more prosperous in Judea. Galileans were poor, as a general rule, and Joseph probably had little more means than he needed to make a living. Yet he managed to take Mary and Jesus to Jerusalem every year for Passover (Luke 2:41). He and Mary also went back to the city to search for Jesus when, at twelve, he astounded the temple scholars (Luke 2:46-50).

Obedient under the guidance of Mary and Joseph, Jesus "grew in wisdom and stature, and in favor with God and men" (Luke 2:52). It is likely that Joseph was living when Jesus began his ministry, since in his hometown the Lord is referred to as "the carpenter's son" (Matthew 13:55); but he was probably dead by the time of the crucifixion, since Jesus gave his mother to John (John 19:26-27).

What is missing in our picture of Joseph is any knowledge of his inner life. What were his hopes and dreams for himself and Mary before God intervened? Whatever they were, we only know that he gave precedence to caring for Mary and for God's Son. Perhaps Jesus recalled, in part, his earthly father, Joseph, when he said, "Greater love has no one than this, that he lay down his life for his friends" (John 15:13).

John the Baptist (Luke 3:1-20; John 1:15-36; 3:22-36)

There he was, at last! John must have stopped all speech and action for a moment, seeing his cousin Jesus standing before him at the Jordan, requesting baptism.

John's friendship with Jesus and his adoration of him as the Christ began before either of them was born, for ". . . when Elizabeth heard Mary's greeting, the babe leaped in her womb, and Elizabeth was filled with the Holy Spirit" (Luke

1:41). John, whom God had already singled out for a unique ministry as the one who would prepare the world for its Savior, leaped with recognition of God Incarnate, even while he was in the womb.

John might have grabbed greatness for himself. His followers were devoted, and many were eager to call him Messiah; but he cried, "He who comes after me surpasses me because he was before me" (John 1:15); and when the Jews of Jerusalem sent priests and Levites to ask him who he was, he freely confessed, "I am not the Christ" (John 1:20).

After his baptism of Jesus, John knew that his ministry of preparation was ended and that he must remove himself from the picture. His words to his disciples are possibly the most selfless ever spoken about friendship:

> "The bride belongs to the bridegroom. The friend who attends the bridegroom waits and listens for him, and is full of joy when he hears the bridegroom's voice. That joy is mine, and it is now complete. He must become greater; I must become less" (John 3:29-30).

Andrew: Friend and Brother (Matthew 4:18; 10:2; John 1:35-44; Acts 1:13)

Andrew and his brother Simon Peter were from Bethsaida, a town on the Sea of Galilee. The two were sons of John, or Jonas, and probably both were followers of John the Baptist (John 1:40). Andrew was the disciple who brought the boy's lunch of loaves and fishes to Jesus when the five thousand needed to be fed (John 6:8), and he was part of a private discussion about the Second Coming (Mark 13:3-4). Tradition tells us that after the resurrection, Andrew preached in Scythia—probably northern Turkey—and that somewhere in Greece, he was crucified on an X-shaped cross. Andrew is the patron saint of Scotland, and his cross is one of the two in the flag of the United Kingdom.

Andrew's importance as a friend of Jesus is based not only on his ministry after the resurrection but also on the fact that he was the first missionary:

> . . . John was there . . . with two of his disciples. When he saw Jesus passing by, he said, "Look, the Lamb of God!"
> When the two disciples heard him say this, they followed Jesus.
> . . . Andrew, Simon Peter's brother, was one of the two who heard what John had said. The first thing Andrew did was to find

his brother Simon, and tell him, "We have found the Messiah" (John 1:35-37, 40-41).

Andrew wanted to share Jesus with his brother; so he said, "I'll get Peter!" when Jesus called him. Andrew could have kept his friendship with Jesus all for himself; he knew that Peter was an outgoing man of great strength and passion who possibly could become very important in the Messiah's expected kingdom. Yet, like Mary and like John the Baptist, Andrew had thoughts, not for himself, but for someone he loved. Sharing Jesus with one's closest friend, brother, or sister without thinking of one's own status is the very essence of Christian love.

Simon Peter: The Man Who Denied His Friend (Matthew 16:13-18; John 13:31-38; 18:25-27; 21:15-18; Acts 2)

Peter was the kind of man others sometimes call a fool or a clown. Although his ability to respond quickly with passion was the source of Peter's strength, it was also sometimes his downfall. Capable of saying, "You are the Christ of God" (Luke 9:20), he also sometimes spoke without thinking, as he did on the Mount of Transfiguration when he was so bewildered that he mentioned building three tabernacles. God had to say, "Listen!" (Luke 9:33).

There are a few acts that can end a deep friendship, and disloyal denial is the worst of them. Yet, although Peter denied Jesus three times, the resurrected Jesus appeared to him and spoke to all the disciples about forgiveness of sins (John 20:23).

On the beach at Galilee Jesus spoke of unconditional love (*agape*) and Peter responded with the affection of friendship (*phileo*). Jesus (who always accepts us where we are) finally shifted to Peter's own language:

> When they had finished breakfast, Jesus said to Simon Peter, "Simon, son of John, do you love me (*agapas*) more than these?" He said, "Yes, Lord; you know that I love you" [*philo*]. . . . A second time he said to him, "Simon, son of John, do you love me" [*agapas*]? He said to him, "Yes, Lord, you know that I love you" (*philo*). . . . He said to him the third time, "Simon, son of John, do you love me" [*phileis*]? Peter was grieved because he said to him the third time, "Do you love me?" And he said to him, "Lord, you know everything; you know that I love you" [*philo*] (John 21:15-17, RSV; Nestle Greek text).

It is interesting to note that after Pentecost, when Peter's wayward tongue was transformed by the fiery presence of the Holy Spirit, Peter never again used *phileo* to mean love. Peter let his idea of friendship be changed into the unconditional and forgiving love that Christ offered him.

James and John: Sons of Thunder (Matthew 4:21-22; Mark 9:1-13; 10:35-45; Acts 12:1-2; Revelation 22:8)

For some reason, James and John (especially John) are often portrayed as being very young, weak, and even rather effeminate. But what did Jesus say about them? He called them *"Boanerges,"* or "Sons of Thunder" (Mark 3:17). In the Hellenized thought of first-century Israel, thunder was God's voice speaking from heaven; and the "Sons of Thunder" were the fast, powerful lightning and supernatural fire that appeared on the earth. So Jesus seems to have implied that two fishermen, James and John, sons of Zebedee and Salome, were powerful men, filled with the voice from heaven. They had speed and light and warmth and strength of purpose. They were probably also muscular and physically strong, since their occupation included maneuvering a boat and pulling in immense fishnets.

These two were among the first disciples called. They went with Jesus to the mountain of the transfiguration (Matthew 17:1; Mark 9:2; Luke 9:28) and were witnesses to his agony in Gethsemane (Matthew 26:37; Mark 14:33).

James is rarely mentioned alone but usually is described in company with John, his friend and brother. Since the Gospel writers do not put many words into the mouth of James, we don't actually know much about his personality. In fact, his brother John does not mention him at all! What we do know is that James followed Jesus immediately when he was called to "catch men" and that he was highly trusted. James was present with Peter, Andrew, and John when our Lord explained some of his more cryptic statements, such as his remarks about Elijah (Matthew 17:9-13). These three were given an account of the Second Coming in Mark 13, and James and John were the two whose passion for Christ impelled them to say, "Shall we call down fire from heaven?" on a village in Samaria that had rejected the Gospel by refusing to welcome Jesus (Luke 9:54-56).

James was one of those who saw the ascension. Since he

was in the Upper Room on Olivet with Jesus' mother and the other disciples (Acts 1:12-26), we can assume he was among the first to be empowered by the Holy Spirit at Pentecost. Later, the love and friendship James had for Jesus was put to the ultimate test, when he was beheaded for his faith by Herod Agrippa (Acts 12:2).

James's brother John cared for Jesus in a very special way. Probably once a follower of John the Baptist, he followed Jesus readily. He helped Peter prepare the last Passover meal, and he leaned against Jesus at Supper, apparently knowing that soon his Friend would be torn away. He must have been the only one who stayed awake when the others fell asleep in Gethsemane, because he wrote every word of the high priestly prayer (John 17). He stood at the foot of the cross, received Jesus' mother as his own, and was one of those who ran to the tomb at the behest of Mary Magdalene. John referred to himself as "the disciple Jesus loved" in the moving portrait of Jesus that we call the Gospel According to John.

In the first of the three epistles attributed to John, the disciple gives us a true picture of friendship, starting with his own intimate acquaintance with Christ. He reminds us that Jesus was real, that the Word of God was visible and touchable. He also reminds us that Jesus was somebody we can call a friend and that we may, no, *must* live in Christian friendship together. This was his purpose when he wrote:

> It was there from the beginning; we have heard it; we have seen it with our own eyes; we looked upon it, and felt it with our own hands; and it is of this we tell. Our theme is the word of life. This life was made visible; we have seen it and bear our testimony; we here declare to you the eternal life which dwelt with the Father and was made visible to us. What we have seen and heard we declare to you, so that you and we together may share in a common life, that life which we share with the Father and his Son Jesus Christ. And we write this in order that the joy of us all may be complete (1 John 1:1-4, NEB).

Although James, the older of the *Boanerges*, went to be with Christ soon after the ascension, John, "the beloved disciple," had to wait to be reunited with the Lord. He became the bishop of Ephesus; later from the island of Patmos, he wrote to the seven churches in Asia of his revelation. Although for some time scholars have said that John the disciple could not possibly have written the biblical pieces attributed to him, recent scholarship suggests that he probably did write every word of the Gospel of John, the epistles, and the book of Revelation. In this last great document, John, the Son of Thunder, wrote about the lightning that will be loosed on earth and described the Lamb's ultimate friendship toward his followers in the last tick of time.

Stephen the Deacon: Friend of His Persecutors (Acts 6–7)

When Stephen was chosen to help distribute food to the poor, he was called "a man full of faith and of the Holy Spirit" (Acts 6:5). A few verses later, we find him described as "a man full of God's grace and power" (6:8). He performed many signs and miracles and was finally brought before the Sanhedrin by members of the Synagogue of the Freedmen.

Stephen showed these Pharisees and legalists exactly how much grace, power, and faith were within him when he offered them salvation, preaching a sermon to all who would listen. To make the truth palatable to his persecutors, Stephen took the typically Jewish route of reviewing all history from Abraham to Moses.

"You stiff-necked people, with uncircumcised hearts and ears!" he cried at his sermon's end (7:51). "You always resist the Holy Spirit—and now you have killed Jesus, too."

At this, his prosecutors "gnashed their teeth at him," but he would not forsake their chance for salvation in exchange for saving himself. He continued to hope for their redemption, speaking to them of his friend, Jesus Christ, at the right hand of God. As the stones began to fly, Stephen continued to offer salvation to those who persecuted him, revealing his vision; and as he "fell asleep," he cried, "Lord, do not hold this sin against them." Like Jesus, Stephen knew that Christian love cannot be killed so easily.

Philip and the Ethiopian (Acts 8:26-40)

Friendships in Christ are not always active forever. Sometimes we meet one another briefly before going on with our individual journeys, yet we make deep marks on each others' faith and life. Thus it was with Philip and the Ethiopian eunuch.

Philip got a message from God that told him to take the road south of Jerusalem toward Gaza. On this route he met a eunuch, an official of the Ethiopian queen. This castrated official, probably a freed slave who rose to power in his country's court, had "gone to Jerusalem to worship, and on his way home was sitting in his chariot, reading the book of Isaiah the prophet" (Acts 8:27-28).

We don't know how far the eunuch got in his attempt to worship. The Law forbade any man blemished by castration to enter the congregation (Deuteronomy 23:1), and it would have been out of the ordinary for a devout Jewish Christian like Philip even to speak to such a person, much less spend any time in friendship. Yet Philip ran up to the chariot of the Ethiopian and explained the passage "He was led like sheep to the slaughter . . ." (Isaiah 53:7). Then he went on to tell him the Good News. Perhaps in his compassionate love, Philip took the eunuch a little further in the prophet Isaiah's writings to this passage:

> For this is what the LORD says:
> "To the eunuchs who keep my Sabbaths,
>   who choose what pleases me
>   and hold fast my covenant—
> to them I will give within my temple and its walls
>   a memorial and a name
>   better than sons and daughters;
> I will give them an everlasting name
>   that will not be cut off."
>
> —Isaiah 56:4-5

Whatever Philip told him, the Ethiopian was convinced that Jesus fulfilled the Old Testament prophecies of Messiah and Savior; when they saw water, the eunuch asked, "Can't I be baptized, here and now?"

So they went down into the water, this Christian and his Ethiopian friend, and the baptism took place; and "when they came up out of the water, the Spirit of the Lord suddenly took Philip away, and the eunuch did not see him again, but went on his way rejoicing" (Acts 8:39).

This brief story illustrates the necessity of being open to God's calling and the importance of ignoring worldly legalisms or prejudices against anyone, be they eunuchs, black Ethiopians, women, or people with handicaps. The story also shows us that we sometimes must "disappear" from the life of a friend whom we have helped into salvation so that the glory of that person's life may go to God.

Ananias: Paul's First Christian Friend (Acts 9:10-19)

Saul was glad to hold the coats of the men who stoned Stephen to death, and afterward he went from house to house, dragging to prison men and women who professed Christ. As a result, the apostles were scattered throughout Judea and Samaria.

Finally, Saul, "still breathing out murderous threats against the Lord's disciples" (Acts 9:1), started for Damascus to find members of the notorious cult of Christians there and take them to Jerusalem to prison. But on the way he was invited into friendship by Jesus Christ—and struck blind by the event!

At this point Ananias, a faithful follower of the Way, was called by God to restore Saul's sight.

Ananias was startled. "Are you sure you have the right man, Lord? Has it escaped your attention that Saul has been arresting—"

"Go! This man is my chosen instrument," said God (9:15); and Ananias faithfully obeyed. When he arrived at the house on Straight Street, he let Christ transform his human feelings as he addressed Saul: "Brother Saul, the Lord . . . has sent me, that you may see again and be filled with the Holy Spirit" (9:17).

We may also assume that Ananias baptized Saul, since the next verse tells us that as soon as "something like scales" fell from the Pharisee's eyes, he got up and was baptized (9:18).

Perhaps the story of Ananias is given to us as an example of how, when we are friends with Christ, we become able to love even those who have been our enemies.

Paul of Tarsus: The Man Who Risked Everything (Acts 9, 13-28)

It is impossible in this space to do a real in-depth study on the person I feel was Christ's greatest New Covenant friend, Paul of Tarsus. This is not because there is so little material but because there is enough in Scripture and tradition about Paul to fill great libraries; all of this book could be taken up with describing just his love for God and for his Christian brothers and sister.

I would commend to the reader the fourteenth, fifteenth, and sixteenth chapters of Paul's letter to the Romans as a portrait of Paul himself, as an index of behavior for Christian friends, as a portrait of Paul the friend, and as a partial list of the women and men Paul loved and the favors he begged for them.

It is important to remember that Paul always wanted to be a friend to God. He was a Jew, a devout Pharisee, and a privy counselor to the Sanhedrin. His zealous mistreatment of Christians came out of his belief that God hated them.

We find him first as "a young man named Saul" watching the cloaks of those who stoned Stephen to death, giving his assent to the execution (Acts 7:58; 8:1). Immediately—as if a taste of blood brought out the beast in him—Saul began to persecute the church in Jerusalem. The Christian organization was in disarray; all except the apostles had fled, scattered through Judea and Samaria, while Saul began a house-to-house search for Christians (8:2-3).

God could have destroyed Saul or made him powerless by protecting the Christians. The desperate church probably thought that the Almighty could have done a thousand things other than what was done; but heavenly ways are not our ways. God called Saul to be the "chosen instrument" and greatest of the apostles, even as he was journeying to Damascus to arrest Christians:

> As he neared Damascus on his journey, suddenly a light from heaven flashed around him. He fell to the ground and heard a voice say to him, "Saul, Saul, why do you persecute me?"
> "Who are you, Lord?" Saul asked.
> "I am Jesus, whom you are persecuting," he replied. "Now get up and go into the city, and you will be told what to do" (Acts 9:3-6).

For the rest of his life, Saul-become-Paul did what he was told to do. He journeyed all over the Hellenic world, preaching the gospel of salvation by faith, not to the Jews (as he had supposed he would do), but to the Gentiles (Acts 13:46-48). He was repeatedly imprisoned and flogged, receiving the "thirty-nine lashes" five times. He was beaten with rods, stoned once (and left for dead), shipwrecked three times, tossed for a day and a night in the open sea, and exposed to constant danger from bandits, Jews, Gentiles, and false brothers. He said, "I have been in danger from rivers . . . in danger in the city, in danger in the country, in danger at sea. . . ." He labored and toiled, went without sleep or food, and was sometimes cold and naked (2 Corinthians 11:23b-27). Yet this converted

Pharisee said, "Be joyful always, pray continually, give thanks in all circumstances, for this is God's will for you in Christ Jesus" (1 Thessalonians 5:16-18).

Paul risked much for Jesus. First, he risked having a home. He began his life as an apostle when he was a young man, and he probably never married, for what wife would have put up with this Christian Ulysses? He risked reputation, making himself vulnerable to scorn and ridicule, in order to take the gospel to the world. He risked all other relationships, for Paul was abrasive in his insistence on the purity of the Good News—not currying the favor of men and women, but seeking to do God's perfect will. He certainly risked life and safety, as we have seen, for his friendship with Jesus Christ, and yet he gave thanks in all circumstances.

10

Personal Relationship with Jesus Christ: The Ultimate Friendship

> *What a Friend we have in Jesus,*
> *All our sins and griefs to bear. . . .*
> *Can we find a friend so faithful,*
> *Who will all our sorrows share? . . .*
> *In his arms he'll take and shield thee,*
> *Thou wilt find a solace there.*
> —Joseph Scriven, 1819–1866

On the last evening before he was to die, Jesus washed his disciples' feet.

"He had always loved those who were his in the world, but now he showed how perfect his love was," says the beloved disciple (John 13:1, *The Jerusalem Bible*). Jesus, the complete embodiment of friendship, washed his followers' feet as a final act of earthly love between himself and them. And even though he knew that Judas was going to betray him within the hour, Jesus washed his feet, too.

The Jerusalem Bible translation is especially lovely in this passage. ". . . Now he showed how perfect his love was" isn't just a pretty line of poetry; it is the fulfillment of Jesus' friendship. The King of love knelt before his friends—and an enemy—and cleansed their feet.

This is the first great element of Jesus' friendship with us: *He loves us perfectly, unconditionally, even when we are less than faithful to him.* Through his words and his ministry Jesus gives himself as friend and as example for friendship.

"Who is this Jesus? What is he?" are questions that have echoed throughout history. Why does he wash our feet and forgive our sins and offer us eternal life? Just who is this friend Jesus?

Truly God, Yet Truly a Man

We might begin to answer this question by reviewing the Nicene Creed, the statement of faith made by all Christian leaders at the Council of Nicea in A. D. 325. This basic Christian statement declares that Jesus is Lord, that he is God from God, Light from Light, true God from true God. Jesus, says this creed, is the Son—begotten, not made; and the creed reminds us that for us and for our salvation Jesus came down from heaven, and was made man.

The crux of God's love and friendship with us lies in the words "and was made man." Up to that point, you might say, "Sure, Jesus was perfect, but he was God." Mention the incarnation in complete terms, including the fact that Jesus was as much a man as he was God, however, and you're stuck with the fact that his body was much more than a veil of flesh to hide God. Although Jesus was truly God, he was also truly man, that is, truly human, with all the limitations of human existence. He became what we are so that we would never be alone again, even in grief, poverty, pain, or despair. When we suffer for him, he suffers with us.

When I talk about the incarnation, I am always reminded of my friend Leone's story about her seven-year-old nephew. He was a child who heard robbers and bears in his closet at night. When the lights were out, monsters cavorted under his bed. Fierce, night-loving gorillas were undoubtedly the cause of the rustling in the trees that grew in front of the bedroom window. This was a boy who wasn't spoiled; he was really scared, really shaking in his little bed!

No matter what his parents did for him, he was genuinely scared every night, and someone had to go sit in the room until he fell asleep.

One night when his parents had to go to a meeting, Aunt Leone stayed with him. He had a particularly hard time falling asleep that night.

"Remember, honey, God is always in the room with you," she finally reminded him, as she stood in the doorway to his bedroom.

"Maybe so," the boy yelled desperately, "but I need something with skin on it!"

We might laugh, but we can all relate to this child's fears and needs. Humanity does, indeed, need something or someone who is visible and warm and touchable. God sent us that "something with skin" in the person of Jesus Christ. Eager to show love, God became human. Jesus could offer no greater friendship than stepping off the throne to become a helpless little baby for the sake of all who were helpless.

Sorrow Becomes a Crucible

"I am your friend," says Jesus. "Do you want to love me in return? Then prepare yourselves to suffer."

The second truth about Christ's friendship for us is this: *To accept the compelling love of Jesus and to strive to return it is to ask for suffering.* Life with Jesus is the kind of commitment that leaves us totally changed. Someone might sometimes even look back and think, "It was all easier, simpler, before I became a Christian."

Loving Jesus was no easier when he walked on earth than it is now. All someone had to do was say that he or she wanted to follow him, and he would list the hard conditions that a true relationship with him brings: "Foxes have holes, and birds of the air have nests, but the Son of Man has nowhere to lay his head" (Matthew 8:20). "I am sending you out like sheep among wolves" (Matthew 10:16). "Whoever wants to be first must be slave of all" (Mark 10:44). "You will be handed over to the local councils and flogged from the synagogues" (Mark 13:9). "Do you think I came to bring peace on earth? No, I tell you, [not peace] but division" (Luke 12:51). "If the world hates you, keep in mind that it hated me first" (John 15:18).

Yet, although Jesus' promises of persecution and hatred might discourage those whose love for him is frail, there have always been others who found him impossible to resist. In fact, sorrow was, and is, the crucible in which true faith was—and still is—tried. Knowing that they faced criticism and rejection, knowing that hardship was ahead, knowing that they might be put to death for their friendship with Christ, the disciples went with him from Galilee to Judea and then to his ascension from the Mount of Olives. And in the early Church, no matter how many fell away, there were still those who went to the whip or the lions or the stake, singing his praises.

Although most of us won't ever face being flogged or burned at the stake for our friendship with Jesus, he still asks for everything. He's always asking me to be kind to someone who's horrid, to give my spending money to charity, or to bandage up a neighbor child's hurt kitty even if I feel like throwing up. Jesus sends me places I don't want to go, making me look at life situations that are unbearable, asking me to minister to someone who seems past any help. But I don't go alone; he is part of every hospital call, every consolation visit, every basket of food delivered. The hard part of all this is not the physcial effort of calling or delivering; the emotional involvement with others and the spiritual involvement with him are what make these things a dying to self.

Total Emptying

In the process of suffering and having our egos crushed, we discover the third element of friendship with the Lord: *To be filled with the love of Jesus, we must empty ourselves of everything*. There isn't room for self when the love of Christ takes over our lives, and we need to go through that process called "kenosis," or self-emptying, just as Jesus emptied himself of godhood (Philippians 2:7, RSV).

To empty ourselves is to give up all we have. Jesus described this perfectly when he saw the widow put her tiny coin in the offering. He said, "The others all gave out of wealth; but she, out of her poverty, put in everything—all she had to live on" (see Luke 21:4).

Ours is a Lord who doesn't want the sacrifice of bulls and goats; neither does he want the kind of easy charity that demands little from us. He desperately pleads that we, like the widow, give everything; he wants us to be "poor in spirit" so that he can give us the kingdom of heaven, filling us with his loving friendship. He wants our giving to tax us, to drain us, so that he can say of you and me, "She (or he) put in everything."

When Scripture says that it is a terrible thing to fall into the hands of the living God (Hebrews 10:31), it understates just how awesome God's presence in daily life can become. The whole personality is at risk, because relationship with Jesus will inevitably change us completely. The question "Have you counted the cost?" is answered in having our own egos submerged in the personality of Jesus himself. "In the same way, any of you who does not give up everything he has cannot be my disciple," says Jesus (Luke 14:33).

Centuries of being submerged in hot, silica-laden water changed some ancient trees into the rocks we call "petrified wood." Every cell of these fallen trees was occupied by minerals until the minerals took over the structure. Friendship with the Lord is something like this transformation. The Holy Spirit comes to dwell within us, transforming us, changing us more and more into the likeness of Jesus Christ.

Friendship with Jesus Leads to Friendship with Others

At this point, we encounter the fourth principle of friendship with Jesus: *To let Jesus become our friend is to let him make us into friends to others.* In fact, the very moment I say, "Jesus, will you be my friend?" he is not only deepening the relationship between us, but he is also already laying groundwork within me to become a better friend to people around me.

Jesus' way of being a friend is impeccable. From the beginning of his life on earth, there was a constant flow of perfection in his human relationships because he was in obedience to the voice of God. Because his yea was yea and his nay, nay, liars looked him in the face and suddenly spoke truth. Thieves returned money, slatterns became upright women who anointed his feet, and a band of unlettered Galileans became the central force in history.

In the Sermon on the Mount Jesus offers us a friendship recipe containing the yeast of ethical and spiritual action. This leaven, this yeast (as in Matthew 13:33) lightens the loaf of human interaction.

"Think of others first," he says. "Offer the other cheek; walk the second mile."

"Be the salt that has not lost its saltiness," says Jesus, "the light that isn't hidden. And let your behavior glorify God, not yourself. Don't be false; don't pretend to be pious or a faithful tither if you have murderous thoughts or judge your fellow man or woman to be a fool, a failure, someone unworthy of your attention. Don't bring God your offering when you've left a trail of hurt somewhere; don't pride yourself on purity when you're looking at your neighbor's spouse with lustful thoughts. You're no better than your thoughts are at any given moment!"

He also calls us to expect a great deal from ourselves. "Be perfect, even as God is perfect," he says; but on the other hand, he calls us to accept others without judgment. "Walk a narrow path yourself, but don't judge someone else's sin," he says. "Build your house on the rocks of practice, not on the sand of hearing only."

These are wonderful words of life. In this collection of pithy sayings, Jesus sums up all the qualities that he has and asks us to have them as well. He wants us to be friends who are more than fair; he asks us to be *just*, which is much more. Fairness is humanity's ethic; justice is God's and is much more difficult to attain. Our human sense of "fairness" would make everybody equal at birth and let those who fall down on the path to God stay down. But God's justice is beyond human terms; it asks us to walk a narrow path while judging nobody else and to be perfect in spite of our weaknesses, while giving assistance to the others who are weak. Human fairness would make heaven impossible because we would have to deserve it, but God's justice sends us to heaven because Jesus fulfilled the law for all of us, for all time.

Christ's kind of friendship asks us to be to others what he is to us. He became what we are—and asks us to share the joys and struggles of others, but not from the remote position of charity.

If I take a lemon pie to a bereaved friend, that's charity. If I stay for an hour and hold her in my arms while she cries, that's more like love. And if I stay all afternoon, help her scrub her kitchen floor, yell with her when anger overtakes her, and cry with her in terrible grief, I can actually become part of her suffering in the same way that Christ is part of *my* every weakness.

I learned this lesson one day when my pastor, who was sick in bed, asked me to go over to the city jail and visit a man he was helping—a very young man, incarcerated for theft. I hate this kind of calling; but I went because I knew that nobody else on the church crisis team liked it any better than I did (and besides, Jesus was nudging me, as usual). I was even more frustrated when I realized that the prisoner and I would have to look at each other through a heavy glass window and speak through telephones.

Suddenly, as we were trying to work our way through some conversation, he began to cry because he believed himself to be the worst person on earth.

It was terrible: great sheets of water began to cover his cheeks, and racking sobs shook his body. He was too choked to speak, and at that point so was I. I couldn't even touch his hand in friendship, because of the wall of glass that authority had erected between us. So I started to cry, too. I put my palm against the glass and wept; he placed his hand against the window where mine was, and we cried together for about five or ten minutes. I cried out of frustration, because I couldn't do anything for this sorrowing man; he cried because he believed that he was completely bad.

I reported to my pastor that I had made the call and that it was a total disaster.

"Don't ever send me over there again!" I told him apologetically. "I have absolutely no talent for that sort of thing."

Twinkling, he said, "As a matter of fact, I do want you to go back. When I visited the young man today, he said you were the only person who had ever seemed to understand him in his whole life."

"But—I couldn't even talk," I said.

"I guess that's the secret. He's been talked to death. There are plenty of psychiatrists and social workers; so he doesn't need another professional helper," the pastor told me. "And he's been chewed out by his family and the authorities, so he doesn't need someone to scold or tell him that God said not to steal. Whatever you did over there, you touched his life." I had, accidentally and through the grace of God, given the man all I had at the time—and that is what Jesus asks us for: not what we want to give, not what's feasible to give, not what we think we can give. He asks us to give all of ourselves.

In his ministry among the people Jesus asked his followers to love others with the same degree of care that they give their own bodies and souls and to offer more than they were asked for in both friendship and business.

But on the last night with the disciples, at the Passover

table, things changed. Having given the example of friendship in foot washing, he asked for more, much more. In a passage already studied in an earlier chapter of this book, Jesus asked that we love one another as he has loved us. And then, for perhaps the first time, he called the people who have followed him "friends."

> "My command is this: Love each other as I have loved you. . . . You are my friends if you do what I command. I no longer call you servants, because a servant does not know his master's business. Instead, I have called you friends, for everything that I learned from my Father I have made known to you. You did not choose me, but I chose you to go and bear fruit—fruit that will last. Then the Father will give you whatever you ask in my name. This is my command: Love each other" (John 15:12-17).

Can we love each other the way Jesus loves us? He was willing to lay down his life, not for the deserving just, but for the sinful. For us.

The answers may be found in the fact that although we may believe that we made a conscious decision for Christ, he chose us first from the foundations of the world. He chose us and called us and then gave us the freedom to come or to run away. And if we come to him, he lets the Holy Spirit transform and empower us for that "laying down of life."

Taking Part in the Great Masquerade

Until that transformation by the Holy Spirit is completed, we live out the last great law of friendship with Jesus: *We are asked to participate in what I call "The Great Masquerade."* "Rather, clothe yourself in the Lord Jesus Christ," says Paul in Romans 13:14, after denouncing drunkenness, immorality, dissension, and jealousy. Note that he doesn't say "act like Christ" or "think like Christ." He says that we should clothe ourselves, put on Christ as a garment. This calls us to wear the costume, not of self-righteousness, but of Christ, the Lamb of God; Paul goes on to call it "the armor of light." This costume isn't made from the fabric of ego-gratification, Paul insists. Pretending to be the Lord Jesus Christ is one more action that requires self-emptying.

What? Is Paul crazy? How can we take part in such a disguise and be selfless, transparent Christians at the same time?

The answer is available only to those who are brave enough to try on this "clothing." Immediately, we discover that these are garments with power—the power of death and resurrection. To put on Christ is to ask God to change us into the likeness of Jesus. Our own personalities are buried, changed, covered by this clothing we wear. It is as Scripture says, "For you died, and your life is now hidden with Christ in God" (Colossians 3:3).

Once having begun the process of transformation by putting on Christ, we complete the Great Masquerade by seeing only Christ in all our brothers and sisters, too!

". . . All of you who were baptized into Christ have been clothed with Christ," proclaims Galatians 3:27-28. "There is neither Jew nor Greek, slave nor free, male nor female, for you are all one in Christ Jesus." If we take this Scripture seriously, we have no right to look for anything except the Lord Jesus himself in others who wear this heavenly clothing. Petty squabbles, personality quirks, jealousy, and immense personal opinion suddenly become vague in our sight—perhaps even invisible. In fact, church schisms, arguments over doctrine or liturgy, and even the suspicion of heresy could all be hidden under this garment of Christ, which is woven with unconditional love.

In fact, the masquerade tends to extend itself to all people, not just other Christians. Love is never in short supply, and there's plenty to go around to everyone, since all were created by God. Besides, hungry and thirsty people, prisoners, and all kinds of sufferers might be the King himself in disguise. According to Matthew 25:31-46, we are subject to God's wrath or pleasure by how we treat these perhaps unlovable sojourners.

This Great Masquerade that comes through friendship with Jesus changes every other friendship. It may send us to share suffering we can't ease or to experience joy for another's success. To clothe oneself in Christ and to see this same Garment on everyone else, tends to make us realize how much we are connected to other human beings. C. S. Lewis calls this connection "one huge organism, like a tree."[1]

You will never be left alone in your effort to attend this Great Masquerade. Christ himself is always at your elbow, pleading, urging, tenderly helping; and the Holy Spirit indwells you so that one day the inside will match the Clothing you wear. For

[1] C. S. Lewis, *Mere Christianity* (New York: Macmillan, Inc., 1964), p. 159.

when God asks us for everything, God also gives everything in return; and we call the Everything that God gave, Jesus Christ. The ultimate Friend.

Friendship with Jesus is habit-forming. We come to him for pardon and salvation; we stay with him for renewal and relationship, and soon we are calling others to his Way. This is what makes Christianity different from some other religions: Jesus offers himself rather than creating a doctrine. He comes as Substitute and Savior and stays beside us forever, the complete friend for all seasons; for our religion is a Person, not a belief system. Jesus the Friend is always truthful, sometimes abrasive, unconditionally loving, always warm and open. He confronts us in our misdoings, strengthens us in trouble, raises our hopes when we are discouraged, and puts up with our foolishness. He is the sign to a broken world that God is love.

11

Prayer Partners and Spiritual Friends

And I pray that you, being rooted and established in love, may have power, together with all the saints, to grasp how wide and long and high and deep is the love of Christ . . . (Ephesians 3:17-18).

Kevin and Richard are businessmen who meet for an early restaurant breakfast every Monday morning, with the sole purpose of praying together and counseling each other in their spiritual progress. Their midweek telephone calls are for Christian encouragement. If one of them has a new understanding or a problem with the meaning of a passage of Scripture or a period of either great comfort or unusual dryness in prayer, they pray and talk it over, encouraging each other's spiritual progress.

When Richard had a heart attack three years ago, Kevin kept an all-night prayer vigil in his own home. He also visited the hospital every day for the three weeks of his friend's confinement, praying aloud each time. When Kevin was considering a major change in occupation, Richard fasted and prayed for him, seeking guidance from Scripture and the Holy Spirit. He offered spiritual counsel only, knowing that Kevin had plenty of employment advisors in his business life. Because they attend the same church, their families have a cordial speaking acquaintance, but they rarely, if ever, get together for recreation.

Sally and Teressa are prayer partners, too, but their relationship is somewhat different. They met at a weekly neighborhood Bible study, and each was attracted to the other's commitment to intercessory prayer. After a time, they began getting together after the study every week. They eat a quick lunch and sometimes chat for a few moments about their own needs or problems, offering each other loving support. Each woman has a long list of people who need or have asked for prayer, and they spend about an hour interceding for these needs through "prayer dialogue," in which one prays aloud for her particular concern and then the other adds her vocal prayer for that same concern.

At the end of the time, Sally and Teressa ask God's blessing on each other. They call during the week if an emergency prayer request comes or sometimes just to encourage each other. Their husbands are friends and their children play together; so the two families, unlike Richard's and Kevin's, often get together for informal suppers, picnics, or other outings.

Lee Chin and his wife, Rebecca, meet with Carl and Lisa Martin every other Monday to study the Bible. Carl and Lisa have two children, but the other couple has none; so they usually meet at the Martins's home to avoid the necessity of a baby-sitter. The two women were roommates at Bible college and later worked together in the mission field. They both eventually married busy young pastors who weren't acquainted.

For several years, the two couples saw each other only occasionally until all four people expressed a desire for more in-depth, personal prayer and a study of God's Word, based on the needs of their particular lives. The two ministers both have busy parishes, and they appreciate the feeding they receive in their meetings. Occasionally when a problem arises in their congregations, their marriages, or in some aspect of their personal lives, the four will openly discuss it, exhorting and supporting each other and praying together.

Amanda, a young mother and piano teacher, journeys once monthly to a retreat center about sixty miles from her home. She meets with the center's director, who listens, counsels, and reads the daily prayer journal that Amanda keeps. They usually spend about two hours together, discussing Amanda's spiritual progress and her prayer life and praying together in the chapel. Occasionally, when her cousin can watch her children, Amanda stays overnight, so that they can meet for a longer time. Amanda speaks of the director as "my dearest friend," even though their friendship is limited to a specific time, setting, and purpose.

Craig and Jim meet for prayers together every week. As soon as they have exchanged greetings and hung up their coats, they sit down and read a brief, inspirational passage of Scripture. Then they close their eyes and maintain absolute silence for twenty-five minutes, afterwards discussing the comfort or direction they have experienced. Occasionally—but rarely—one of them has an unusual spiritual insight that he wishes to share, and he speaks aloud during the prayer period; otherwise, their time together is silent. This relationship is simply an opportunity to meditate on God's Word together and to let the Holy Spirit speak to them and through them.

The two men prayed and studied aloud together until Craig brought a booklet in which a man described his first, quieting prayers at a silent Christian meeting: "When I have finished these inward prayers, I quietly resign myself to complete listening—letting go in the intimacy of this friendly company and in the intimacy of the Great Friend who is always near."[1] After they read this material, Craig and Jim decided to try it together. They have now been "in the silence," as some people call this kind of prayer, for several years. They feel very close to God and are highly sensitive to the needs of others since they began praying together this way.

Seven men and women gather every Monday night in the church parlor, as they have for about ten years. They read a Bible lesson from a prescribed course of study and then pray aloud together for about half an hour—for all who have asked for intercessions, for their own congregation, and for the Church in the world. At the end of the time, they join hands and each person prays in turn for the one on his or her right, asking God for health, strength, and the ability to meet all the needs of the coming week.

[1] Douglas V. Steere, *A Quaker Meeting for Worship* (Philadelphia: Philadelphia Yearly Meeting of the Religious Society of Friends, 1980), p.7.

Several of them meet often for lunch, family recreation, or other social occasions, while the others rarely see one another outside their prayer meeting or church services. But since the group members have met together in prayer for so many years, they all have a feeling of close friendship, often lifting one another up in private prayer.

Iris entered rather gradually into spiritual direction with Leslie, a younger friend. One night after a church midweek Bible study that Iris led, Leslie asked the other woman to go to a nearby ice-cream parlor to discuss an important decision she was trying to make. They talked for some time about the matter and about Leslie's prayer life, which was just beginning to blossom. When she called a few days later to tell Iris about the results of her decision, she also invited her to lunch the following week. And so on. Soon they were meeting regularly to talk and pray about growth in the Lord.

These seven friendships are designed to glorify God, to spread the kingdom of heaven through the world, and to uphold each person's prayer life. Important, sensitive, spiritual relationships like these have always existed, but there has been a sudden gain in numbers in the past few years. People are seeking friendships in which they can be open and honest, and which aren't centered on recreation or social activity only.

Most of the relationships that I have written about are devised intentionally. For instance, Richard called Kevin the first time with a spiritual partnership in mind; when they met, they decided to meet regularly for prayer. Amanda asked the retreat-center leader to be her spiritual director after a prayer retreat that she and some friends attended at the center. Rebecca and Lisa and their husbands decided gradually to have a study and prayer time in lieu of any other kind of get-together, since they had plenty of other opportunities to make friends but few for in-depth spiritual advancement.

Some spiritual friendships, however, come together by accident (if anything is ever accidental in God's plan) or casually, as in the case of Iris and Leslie. When they do "happen," it is wise to let them grow at their own pace, because the people in them are probably spontaneous by nature.

When two or more Christian people meet together for prayer, study, and/or spiritual counsel, Jesus is in the midst of them (Matthew 18:20). Because he is the greatest of all friends, he offers himself gladly for those whose friendships are centered in him and is generous to provide his counsel and consolation to all who are thirsty.

Jesus Christ must be the real leader in every group or pair of praying partners so that one human being never puts himself or herself in the dangerous position of spiritual authority over others. Even when one person is in the position of "director," this position has to be taken with humility and gentleness; counsel is given with the understanding that this is a suggestion, not a command.

If you and one or more others want to come together regularly as spiritual friends, design your relationship ahead of time according to everyone's needs, purposes, and goals. Needs and goals can be personal; for instance, one person's goals may be for better understanding of Scripture and more self-discipline in prayer, while his or her partner may be seeking spiritual peace or the "loosening-up" of a Pharisaic nature.

The purpose of your meetings, however, should be the same. You will probably be most comfortable if you covenant this relationship by writing a statement of purpose, such as "We will meet every week to pray together for ourselves and others," or "Marsha, Louise, and Gwen will meet every month to discuss their progress in prayer, to study Scripture, and to read portions of a classic on spirituality." Whatever the purpose is, define the terms carefully so that people don't feel, after a few weeks or months, that they aren't getting what they thought they would. Take plenty of time to listen to all opinions when working out your exact purpose so that your meaning is absolutely clear and each person can express his or her ideas.

You might want to borrow again from our Quaker brothers and sisters, who believe that unanimity is the Holy Spirit expressed. Pray for guidance; then maintain silent prayer for a time; and after that, begin to design the plan for your meetings. If one person is uncomfortable with any part of the plan or doesn't agree to the agenda, then there is no consensus; so, enter into silent prayer again and try once more to find the "inner light" that Quakers tell us about so beautifully.

The reason this is so important is that spiritual friendships must be in God's will, not in the wills of people. If one person exerts his or her will over another reluctant person, the relationship won't work and won't glorify God.

If you aren't positive of exactly what you need or want or

haven't chosen a prayer partner and yet still feel the need for a spiritual relationship, you might respond to the following:

1. Number the following in order of greatest need in your life: (a) Bible study, (b) prayer dialogue, (c) silent community prayer, (d) a chance to be an intercessor, (e) an opportunity to witness, (f) spiritual direction, (g) an opportunity to give spiritual direction, (h) a partner to agree with me in prayer, (i) someone with whom to share love for Christ, (j) someone I can open up with about my inner life.

2. Is there someone I know well or someone I have only met with whom I think could be a spiritual friend?

3. Am I most comfortable praying (a) alone, (b) at church, (c) in groups of three or four, (d) with one other person?

When you have answered these questions, you may have a clearer idea of what you need. If you don't know any person who seems to be right as a spiritual friend in your life, ask your pastor or Bible study leader if he or she knows such a person. You needn't be friends in the common sense of the word; you need only to have the same purpose for your relationship.

Whether yours is a partnership of intercessory prayer or an in-depth searching for spiritual perfection together, make sure that you keep these criteria in mind:

1. Affirm that you are part of one Body, the Body of Christ. This is especially important if you are members of different denominations or have differing theological opinions. It's all right to discuss these differences occasionally as interesting variations, but don't let them come between you as persons. Remember that "you are no longer foreigners and aliens, but fellow citizens with God's people and members of God's household, built on the foundation of the apostles and prophets, with Christ Jesus as the chief cornerstone" (Ephesians 2:19-20).

2. Keep in mind that unity, not discord, is God's loving will for all of us. "In him the whole building is joined together and rises to become a holy temple in the Lord. And in him you too are being built together to become a dwelling in which God lives by his Spirit" (Ephesians 2:21-22).

3. Be gentle. Don't judge one another's progress. Allow yourselves to go at your own paces. One of you may be

spiritually far more advanced or more knowledgeable about Scripture than the other(s), or one may interpret the Word a little differently from the other(s). "Be humble and gentle; be patient, bearing with one another in love" (Ephesians 4:2).

4. Let love guide you. Be open and honest and help one another feel secure about words spoken in confidence. If you're failing miserably at private prayer, don't "show off" in group prayer and don't tell your partner, "Oh, the Lord is doing a great work in me!" On the other hand, do not be harsh with one another's spiritual shortcomings, or else you will discourage one another until your group falls apart. "Instead, speaking the truth in love, we will all grow up into him who is the Head, that is, Christ. From him the whole body, joined and held together by every supporting ligament, grows and builds itself up in love, as each part does its work" (Ephesians 4:15-16).

5. Don't have such a rigid format or such narrow goals that you ignore one another's needs. During a really difficult, lonely period of my life, I regularly attended a no-nonsense Bible study and prayer meeting that was led by a prim young man who drilled us like soldiers. We submitted our list of needs or intercessions to him, and he read them aloud during the prayer time without any explanation. I'm sure God heard my name and need—but nobody in that study ever realized that I was absolutely miserable.

I finally switched to a women's group in which I felt comfortable being open and where I gained great strength from the love and encouragement of my sisters.

Make sure that you care for each other, and be sensitive to each other's needs. "Be imitators of God, therefore, as dearly loved children and live a life of love, just as Christ loved us and gave himself up for us as a fragrant offering and sacrifice to God" (Ephesians 5:1-2).

6. Be careful! Praying and counseling together can sometimes lead to such sensitivity to each other that a few spiritual friendships have become very unspiritual; even where nothing is amiss, others outside the relationship may interpret it wrongfully. Therefore, in cases where only two people are prayer partners, it is usually wisest for men to pray with men and women with women; in larger groups, this isn't as important. It's a sad fact that men and women who came together to pray have sometimes found too late that they were

playing with fire or that their reputations were tarnished. "Be very careful, then, how you live—not as unwise but as wise, making the most of every opportunity, because the days are evil. Therefore, do not be foolish, but understand what the Lord's will is" (Ephesians 5:15-17).

7. Do not let impatience, irritation, misunderstanding, anger, or hostility destroy a relationship that can glorify God. One thing that the enemy hates worse than a praying Christian is two praying Christians! Therefore, the world, the flesh, and the devil may seem to be contending against your spiritual friendship with "fiery darts" of hurt feelings or severe misunderstanding. When bad feelings come up, pray about them aloud, together, immediately; don't let the sun go down on your wrath. Then, together, turn your security in being part of the one Body of Jesus Christ into a full-scale prayer effort. "For our struggle is not against flesh and blood, but against the rulers, against the authorities, against the powers of this dark world and against the spiritual forces of evil in the heavenly realms" (Ephesians 6:12).

8. Always be ready to intercede and pray for the whole Church each time that you meet. Your own spiritual progress is vastly important, but it must never become so parochial that you can't pray for or with anyone else who asks. People who know you as prayer friends will soon bring you their needs for prayer. Even if you aren't partners or a group designed for intercession, pray anyway. There is no higher calling than being an intercessor, for Jesus Christ himself set the pattern for us when he interceded once and for all on our behalf. So, as you grow spiritually, others will ask for your help; when they do, "pray in the Spirit on all occasions with all kinds of prayers and requests. With this in mind, be alert, and always keep on praying for all the saints" (Ephesians 6:18).

It is obvious by now that all these suggestions for partnership came from the letter to the Ephesians, which is one of the great discourses on Christian ethics. I would suggest that as you come together to propose a prayer friendship, you read this epistle together several times for inspiration and for specific direction. And finally, I would like, as a Christian writer, to ask that you

> Pray also for me, that whenever I open my mouth, words may be given me so that I will fearlessly make known the mystery of the gospel, for which I am an ambassador. . . . Pray that I may declare it fearlessly, as I should (Ephesians 6:19-20).